WRITING EXCELLENCE

THE RHETORIC PROGRAM
AT OAKLAND UNIVERSITY

Pearson
Custom
Publishing

Cover Art: "Riverdance," by Angela Sciaraffa.

Copyright © 2002 by Pearson Custom Publishing

Printed in the United States of America

10 9 8 7 6 5 4 3 2 1

Please visit our web site at www.pearsoncustom.com

ISBN 0–536–63763–6

BA 993450

PEARSON CUSTOM PUBLISHING
75 Arlington Street, Suite 300, Boston, MA 02116
A Pearson Education Company

Contents

Introduction

Welcome to the Rhetoric Program at Oakland University.

Writing Excellence is intended to provide students with an explanation of Oakland's courses in academic writing. Rhetoric Program faculty members hope that students will read the information presented here as well as the essays written by others. The purpose of this book is to introduce students to the goals and expectations of the introductory Rhetoric courses at Oakland.

In the Rhetoric Program, the overall goal is to help students develop skills in writing for use in their courses and professional lives: locating, evaluating, and synthesizing information from diverse sources and multiple perspectives; making original and thoughtful contributions to ongoing arguments; and adapting students' own written products to some of the various stylistic and rhetorical conventions of scholarly research. In this volume, the current program goals and courses are described, along with extensive information about the general policies and procedures that apply to the courses. The text includes information about student resources and about the university library.

The largest portion of the book presents the writing of students at Oakland: winners of the Rhetoric Program's Writing Excellence Awards for the past two years. The papers published here won first place awards in several categories, including not only those specific to the Rhetoric Program, but also entries in a category of writing drawn from courses across the curriculum.

Students should find this book a useful resource for their introductory writing experiences at the university.

◆

Program Goals

The goal of the writing program is to introduce students to the reading and writing of academic discourse. In our sequence of courses (for most students, RHT 150 and RHT 160), students have opportunities to develop skills in all types of writing expected in academic situations. In addition, students will learn analytical and critical reading skills through the program. By the end of the sequence of Rhetoric courses students should be able to

- ◆ write conventional, academically acceptable English, showing control of sentence structure, voice, tone and diction
- ◆ analyze a writing situation in terms of audience, topic and purpose
- ◆ state and support a thesis in a sustained discourse
- ◆ read print and electronic sources analytically and critically and integrate those sources in an argument
- ◆ write an extended research essay incorporating multiple sources to support an argumentative, persuasive or critical purpose
- ◆ meet exacting standards of clarity, focus, relevance and form including proper citation and documentation of those sources in some recognized system (MLA or APA format, e.g.)
- ◆ show promise of being able to apply these skills to personal, academic, professional, and public writing

The Rhetoric Program expects that, with these skills in place, students will develop proficiency through more advanced writing courses in Rhetoric as well as in the various departments of the university that will prepare them to write capably for professional and personal purposes.

Course Descriptions

Following are brief catalog descriptions of the writing courses offered in the Rhetoric Program. Additional information, prerequisites and related material may be found in Oakland's undergraduate catalog.

RHETORIC 045, COMMUNICATIONS SKILLS: A small group course introducing new students to the basic language arts skills of reading, writing and speaking needed for success in the university. Graded S/U. Credits earned may not be used to satisfy minimal graduation requirements in any academic program. (For students in the Academic Opportunity Program.)

RHETORIC 102, BASIC WRITING: Developing writing skills including idea generation and invention, organizational strategies, and conventional usage in expository prose. Emphasis on developing fluency and effective writing processes. Placement by referral. May be repeated once for additional credit. Graded S/U.

RHETORIC 104, SUPERVISED STUDY: Tutorial instruction in areas mutually agreed upon by student and instructor such as independent or academic writing projects. May be taken concurrently with other rhetoric courses. May be repeated for up to 8 credits. Graded S/U.

RHETORIC 150, COMPOSITION I: A course emphasizing the rhetorical and stylistic demands of college writing through focus on experiential, expressive and analytic writing. Students learn to generate, organize and develop their ideas and to make choices as writers that are appropriate to the rhetorical situation. A grade of 2.0 or higher must be achieved to advance to RHT 160.

RHT 160, COMPOSITION II: Emphasizes the process of writing in increasingly complex rhetorical situations with focus on developing analytic thinking and problem-solving strategies in writing. Students learn methods of academic research including evaluation and documentation of sources and are expected to create at least one research paper. A grade of 2.0 or higher must be achieved to satisfy the university writing requirement.

RHT 320, PEER TUTORING IN COMPOSITION: Peer tutoring theories and pedagogies, and practical experience in teaching. Work divided between classroom and tutoring assignments. Particularly valuable for majors in the humanities, education, psychology, human services and related fields.

RHT 334, ADVANCED WRITING: ETHNOGRAPHY: Development of analytic and collaborative writing skills in the context of ethnographic study. Emphasis on written analysis in a variety of forms including case study analysis and ethnomethodological investigation. Appropriate advanced writing experience for majors in communication, psychology, anthropology, sociology and political science.

RHT 335, WRITING FOR HUMAN SERVICES PROFESSIONALS: Development of analytical and collaborative writing skills for human services and training and development professionals. Emphasis on written analysis in a variety of forms including letters, memos, problem statements and proposals among others. Experience in writing individually and cooperatively. Class will include writing workshops and group discussions.

RHT 370, SPECIAL TOPICS: Special topics in composition and rhetoric. May be repeated under different subtitles.

RHT 380, PERSUASIVE WRITING: Advanced writing designed to help students develop argumentative and stylistic skill in a variety of rhetorical contexts with application in business, communication, industry and government.

RHT 414, TEACHING WRITING: Examination of and practice in instructional techniques and research in writing pedagogy, and such related issues as assessment and classroom workshops.

Placement Procedures

The following document is distributed to newly admitted students through the Office of New Student Programs and is also made available to students during summer orientation programs:

The goal of the writing program at OU is to help students become capable, confident writers who have the skills needed to complete writing tasks successfully both during the undergraduate years and beyond. Students must complete RHT 160 with a grade of 2.0 or better to meet the university-wide writing requirement for graduation. At many institutions, including Oakland, most students enroll in two semesters of intensive practice in writing to complete the writing requirement successfully.

The Rhetoric Program offers three courses to help students satisfy the writing requirement for graduation: Basic Writing (RHT 102), Composition I (RHT 150), and Composition II (RHT 160). The Program uses a combination of different instruments to assist students with proper placement. The information below will help you understand which course is right for you.

Placement in Basic Writing (RHT 102)

You will be placed in this course if your ACT English score is 15 or below. This course meets in small sections of 18 students or fewer and will provide you with closely supervised experience developing your writing skills with attention to conventional usage and a focus on the writing process.

Placement in Composition I (RHT 150)

You will be placed in this course if your ACT English score is 16 or above, unless you qualify for Composition II (RHT 160) as described below. Rhetoric 150 offers intensive writing practice and will allow you to develop fluency and flexibility in writing. Most students begin with this course.

Placement in Composition II (RHT 160)

Some students can omit RHT 150 and move directly to RHT 160. If you believe you are a strong writer or your situation is described below, there are several ways you may place into Composition II (RHT 160):

1. If you have taken RHT 15O at OU or its equivalent at another school and achieved a grade of 2.0 or better, you are eligible to enroll in RHT 160. The Rhetoric Program staff will check your academic record during the first week of the term to verify your prior experience.

2. If you have taken the MEAP Writing Test in high school and scored at Level 1 (or Proficient), you may register for RHT 160. You must bring your score report to the Rhetoric Program office (316 Wilson) during the first week of classes to verify your placement.

3. If you have taken an Advanced Placement test in English you should arrange to have your scores sent to OU. Oakland University accepts AP results for both the English Composition and Literature and the English Composition and Language exams as follows: For either exam, a score of 3 places students in RHT 160, and scores of 4 or 5 exempt students from RHT 160 and grant 4 credits in English. (AP English scores and uses are under review.)

4. If you submit a portfolio of writing to the Placement Committee of the Rhetoric Program and are judged to be a skilled writer likely to succeed in RHT 160, you will be given permission to enroll in RHT 160. Portfolios should be submitted as soon as possible and preferably at least two weeks prior to orientation and registration. Placement Portfolio instructions are sent to

new students through the Office of New Student Programs and are also available from the Rhetoric Program office (316 Wilson Hall; 248-370-4121).

During the first week of all classes, students provide a brief impromptu writing sample. These samples will be evaluated by instructors and by the Rhetoric Program director, and on the basis of them, students may be required to enroll for 1 credit of supervised tutorial assistance in RHT 104, Supervised Study.

Transfer Students

Transfer students who have completed composition coursework at other institutions should submit their transcripts to the Registrar's office for evaluation. In general, transfer students who have earned 3-5 credits in a composition course may register for RHT 160.

Transfer students who have earned 6 or more credits in college composition courses, including at least one course that involves academic research writing, should submit their transcripts for evaluation. Syllabi may be requested to verify equivalent course content.

Transfer students who believe that they have the skills to demonstrate their proficiency in writing may petition the Proficiency Committee of the Rhetoric Program by submitting a portfolio of writing and requesting exemption from further coursework. Specific directions and a required cover sheet for the Exemption Portfolio are available from the Rhetoric Program office (316 Wilson Hall; 248-370-4121). See the undergraduate catalog for further information.

CLEP Credit for Composition

There are two CLEP examinations in composition, the subject exam in College Composition and the general exam in English composition.

Students who have fewer than 32 credits and who earn a score of 550 or better may use the subject exam in College Composition as equivalent to 4 credits of RHT 150 and may register for RHT 160.

Students who have fewer than 32 credits and who earn a score of 550 or better may use the general exam in English composition to earn 6 elective credits only.

Course Management Information

Attendance policy

The following statement is a uniform policy on attendance for all courses in the Rhetoric Program at Oakland:

> Rhetoric classes are conducted as relatively small workshops so that you, your classmates and your teacher can develop in a community of readers and writers. Your regular attendance is vital because, as a member of this community, you are expected to do in-class writing as well as contribute to class discussions, peer-editing groups and other course activities. Because your full participation is expected, regular class attendance is a course requirement.

The following attendance policies apply to all RHT classes:

1. Teachers understand that unavoidable events occasionally prevent you from attending class—for example, illness, car trouble, or an athlete's "away" game. Therefore, absences are not labeled "excused" or "unexcused," but they are strictly limited.

2. The Rhetoric Program expects that teachers will deduct points from your final grade if you miss more than 3 MWF, 2 TTH, or one evening class. The suggested deductions are .1, .15, or .3 respectively. Please consult your teacher's syllabus for additional details of this policy.

3. Your eligibility to receive a final grade is determined in part by your attendance. Students who miss more than three weeks of class are not eligible to receive a grade above 0.0.

Reminder: If you are taking RHT 150 or RHT 160 and receive a grade below 2.0, you must repeat the course—and achieve a grade of 2.0 or better—to complete OU's writing proficiency requirement.

Grading policy

Course grades are given using Oakland University's numerical grading system, ranging from 4.0 to 1.0 by tenths, and 0.0 for failing work. Grades are given only by the instructor of record for a particular course. Syllabi should explain how course grades are calculated, the relative emphasis given to different assignments and related matters.

Midterm progress reports

Students in all 100-level and 200-level courses are given an indication of their progress sometime around the middle of the term and no later than a week prior to the last day to take an official Withdrawal (W grade), normally the ninth week of the term. Many Rhetoric instructors provide students with a written summary of their grades as of the middle of the term.

Incompletes

The Rhetoric Program follows university rules for giving the grade of Incomplete for courses. In general, incompletes can only be given if circumstances beyond the control of the student occur after the official withdrawal date and preclude timely completion of the work for a course. Student and instructor should agree on the terms under which the work will be completed and evaluated and should complete and sign the University Registrar's form available for this purpose. The form is available from the Rhetoric Program office (316 Wilson Hall) and from the Registrar's office (100 O'Dowd Hall).

Conferences

All faculty are expected to hold regular office hours at times mutually convenient for themselves and for students, and to hold a reasonable number of office hours each week so that students may come in for individual assistance. Instructors should announce their office hours and location at the beginning of each term.

Class cancellations

If a class must be cancelled by an instructor, the program office is notified and posts a sign for students at the classroom door.

In the winter, university officials make decisions about closings, usually very early in the morning or occasionally during the day if a storm begins after classes start. Closings are typically announced on the major radio stations in the area. Students and faculty can also call the university's hot line number, 248-370-2000 to learn if classes have been cancelled. The hot line is the best official source of information for weather-related university closings.

Computer classrooms

The Rhetoric Program offers instruction in two computer classroom facilities in Wilson Hall (rooms 400 and 400A). Students may also meet occasionally in computer classrooms in the university library.

Grievance Procedure for the Department of Rhetoric, Communication and Journalism

The purpose of this document is to set forth a procedure which will permit resolution of student complaints immediately after they arise and in the spirit of cooperation. All complaints must be initiated within sixty (60) days after the student is aware of the circumstances leading to the complaint. ***This policy complies with the time limits set forth in the University Grievance Procedure.***

1. A student who has a complaint about a classroom situation involving an instructor teaching a course under RHT, COM, or

JRN rubrics has recourse to that instructor. Any member of the Department to whom the student makes his/her complaint must send that student directly to the instructor involved.

2. If student and instructor are unable to resolve differences themselves, or if the student finds it impossible to meet with the instructor directly, the student should take his/her **written** complaint to the Program Director. The criteria for the grounds of a grievance shall include evidence of:

   ◆ Systematic unfairness based on ethnic, racial or gender discrimination based on instructor responses to students,

   ◆ Inconsistency in application of instructor's grading policy (i.e. how the final grade is derived),

   ◆ Inconsistency in application of the standard established by the instructor (i.e. clearly differing evaluation criteria brought into play from student to student in the same assignment),

   ◆ A course clearly becoming something other than what was indicated in the syllabus.

   Complaints of grading harshness or the professional evaluation by instructors of classroom presentations or written essays do not constitute sufficient grounds unless clear evidence of above criteria is present.

3. If the director is the faculty member or cannot resolve the student's concern, it shall be referred to the Department Chair. In an attempt to bring the issue to resolution by serving as a mediator, the Chair shall meet with the Program Director first, and then after meeting separately with both the student and the instructor, try to bring them together, if necessary, to reach an agreement.

4. If the chair determines that formal arbitration is needed, an arbitration panel shall be formed, consisting of three (3) people from the university community: one chosen by the student, one by the instructor, and one by the chair. The mediation panel will hold a hearing in the presence of both parties. After that meeting the panel will confer in closed session.

5. If the problem is not resolved by the arbitration panel, the student may then contact the Dean of the College of Arts and Sciences to continue the resolution process.

In the case of grading complaints the panel may suggest the instructor reevaluate the student's work (which may result in raising or lowering the grade), but the panel does not have the power to change grades. Although collegial recommendation carries persuasive weight, ultimately the teacher of record decides the final grade. For other classroom situations, the panel may likewise recommend a resolution but, ultimately, the instructor of record controls his/her classroom. The suggestion of the panel shall be the final stage of departmental action.

Faculty members are also to be guided by the statements on faculty conduct and professionalism contained in the Faculty Agreement. In addition, it should be noted that non-academic concerns, discrimination, and harassment complaints are governed by the *Oakland University Procedure for the Resolution of Student Complaints.*

(Grievance Revised and Approved 3/29/00)

Academic Conduct policy

Oakland University and the Rhetoric Program demand proper academic conduct. Rhetoric courses are designed to help students learn how to design, carry out and report on a research project using outside sources appropriately. The full academic conduct policy of the university is printed in the Undergraduate Catalog, the Schedule of Classes and the Student Handbook. Students are expected to have read it; it will be discussed in Rhetoric classes as well. Plagiarism, the use of the work of another without proper identification and documentation is a most serious academic offense. The charge of plagiarism, if brought by a faculty member, is taken to the University's Academic Conduct Committee. If the charge is sustained, students may be suspended or expelled from the university; other penalties may also be imposed.

Student Resources

Tutorial for credit: Rhetoric 104

Students can receive tutorial help with the work in Rhetoric courses by enrolling in a credit-bearing tutorial (RHT 104) with a faculty member. The credit-bearing tutorial is RHT 104, Supervised Study, and may be required of some students based on first-week impromptus in writing courses. Students may enroll for RHT 104 for 1 credit (30 minutes of tutorial help each week for the semester). RHT 104 is taught by Rhetoric Program faculty members.

Peer tutoring: Academic Skills Center

The Academic Skills Center provides peer tutoring with advanced students trained to tutor in writing. Rhetoric tutoring is generally offered by appointment, but students should check with the Academic Skills Center to learn whether there are drop-in times available for assistance with Rhetoric courses. The Academic Skills Center is located in Room 100 of North Foundation Hall (248-370-4215).

Online writing assistance

There are a number of online writing labs available at the following public Web sites:

Purdue University: *http://owl.english.purdue.edu/*

University of Michigan: *http://www.lsa.umich.edu/swc/OWL/owl.html*

RPI: *http://www.rpi.edu/dept/llc/writecenter/web/index.html*

Additional online writing assistance can be found at the following Website:

http://www.newark.ohio-state.edu/~osuwrite.owls.htm

Disability Support Services

The university maintains an office to assist students with special needs. Advocacy and support services are provided through the Office of Disability Support Services located in 157 North Foundation Hall (248-370-3266, 3268 for TDD). Services include, but are not limited to, priority registration, special testing arrangements, assistive technology, referrals to outside service agencies, assistance in identifying volunteer notetakers, and volunteer readers, assistance with sign language interpreter services and with any general needs or concerns. Students with special needs are encourage to utilize these services.

The University Diversity and Compliance office (148 North Foundation Hall, 248-370-3496) is also available to assist students with disabilities.

Counseling Center

The university offers students personal counseling, testing, psychotherapy and consultations. The Counseling Center is located in the Graham Health Center (248-370-3465). In addition to counseling and psychotherapy, the center can provide evaluations regarding learning problems and disabilities.

English as a Second Language

The Center for American English at Oakland University provides instruction in writing skills for students of English as a second language. For information about courses and programs, students should contact the Department of Linguistics (Room 320 O'Dowd Hall; 248-370-2175).

Library Information

The library faculty provide formal instruction in research procedures, including the on-line catalog, computerized data bases and the Internet for all sections of RHT 160. Students do exercises to practice the research skills taught during the library sessions. The librarians work with students on search skills and the evaluation and appropriate use of sources for research purposes. Rhetoric faculty members are expected to attend the library instructional sessions with their classes.

Library profile and services:

Homepage: *http://www.kl.oakland.edu*

Use this as your starting point for accessing the Voyager catalog, FirstSearch, Lexis-Nexis and other databases. The KL homepage is also your customized gateway to the vast array of resources on the Internet.

Catalog: Voyager System

Voyager is Oakland University Library's own automated online catalog. Use it to find books, journals, sound recordings, government documents and other materials in our collections as well as course reserve materials. You can also use it to place holds and to check your personal library account.

Collections: 688,000 volumes
1.1 million microforms
Approximately 2100 current journal subscriptions
Expenditures for library materials (2000):
$1,205,276.

Special Collections:

Springer Collection of Lincolniana
Hicks Collection of Early Books by Women
James Collection of Books on Folklore and Witchcraft
Bingham Collection of Children's Literature
University Archives

Databases:

Available via the library home page are FirstSearch, including ABI-INFORM, MLA bibliography, PsycLit, ERIC, Medline and many others; Web of Science, a comprehensive citation database to the sciences and technology; Lexis-Nexis Academic Universe; Congressional Universe; Infotrac Searchbank; MathSciNet; Historical Abstracts; America: History and Life. Electronic full-text content collections include electronic journals in Project Muse, Academic IDEAL and JSTOR, and NetLibrary electronic books.

Documents:

Selective Federal and State depository library since 1964.
Over 215,000 government publications in print and microform.

Services:

Proxy server for remote access to electronic collections
Electronic reserves through Voyager system
Circulation of library materials
Course Reserve (at circulation desk)
Reference desk and email reference service
Research Consultations
Computerized database searching
Library and internet instruction
Interlibrary Loans
Assistive technologies

Computer Labs:

South Lab (mixed platform)—35 work-stations for individual use
North Lab (PCs)—30 work-stations for individual use, teaching classes or group sessions

Robotel Classroom (Room 225A; PCs)—25 student workstations networked to 1 instructor workstation for teaching purposes only.

Hours

Day	Library	Reference
Monday–Thursday	8:00AM–11:30PM	8:00AM–10:00PM
Friday	8:00AM–8:00PM	8:00AM–6:00PM
Saturday	9:00AM–8:00PM	9:00AM–7:00PM
Sunday	Noon–11:30PM	Noon–6:30, 7:30–10:00PM

Telephone: (248)370-2471

Research Advice: What to Use When

When in the library, use the reference area workstations to directly access the following tools. When at home or elsewhere, access them through the library's web site at *http://www.kl.oakland.edu*.

For books, government documents, sound recordings, microforms, and journal titles –in short, to find discrete items in the library's collection—use Voyager. To find articles in magazines or journals about particular topics, use Periodical Indexes and Full Text Databases.

Voyager Library Catalog

Use the library catalog *Voyager* to

- ◆ find books, government documents, sound recordings or other items on a particular topic
- ◆ search journal titles (not article titles!) to find out what journals the library has

Available in the library and also from anywhere on the world wide web. Go to the library's home page (*www.kl.oakland.edu*) and click on the *Voyager Library Catalog*.

Periodical Indexes and Full Text Databases

All of the periodical databases to which our library subscribes may be found in the list of current databases. What follows is a selection of the ones most commonly used by Oakland University patrons.

FirstSearch

FirstSearch is accessed from the library's home page.

Useful databases on *FirstSearch* include the following:

◆ *ABI/Inform* for indexing of articles on business and economic (many articles are full text)

◆ *Periodical Abstracts* for a cross-disciplinary database, including popular and academic journals, covering 2000 titles, many of which are available full text (coverage began in 1987)

◆ *WilsonSelectPlus* for full text articles from popular and academic journals, covering 1300 titles across a variety of disciplines (coverage began in 1994)

◆ Other databases in popular disciplines include *PsychInfo, ERIC, Medline,* and others.

Direct interlibrary loan is available from most databases; just make sure first that we don't already own the title you need by searching it in *Voyager. FirstSearch* is available in the library and from home if you are OU faculty, staff, or a currently by clicking on *Infotrac Searchbank.* All 3 databases include partial full text and full-image contents. *GRCG* indexes general interest periodicals and newspaper articles, encyclopedias and other reference material. Covered subject areas include social sciences, general sciences, humanities, business and management, economics and current affairs. *HRCA* indexes health related journals and magazines—including several fulltext nursing journals. Available from home through the OU proxy server.

Lexis/Nexis

This database includes full text articles from journalistic sources around the world; biographical reference sources; full-text law review articles, case law, federal code and state law sources; full-text business sources. It is an excellent source of full text newspaper articles. Emphasis is on current events and the recent past, but many legal materials have deep historical coverage. Available from home through the OU proxy server.

World Wide Web

To assist you in looking for other research materials on the world wide web, the Library includes links to several useful search engines and other sites from its homepage. Particularly useful sites are *Google* (*www.google.com*) and the *Michigan Electronic Library* (mel.org). Remember that web materials, like printed materials, need to be questioned as to accuracy, recency, perspective, and authority.

First Floor

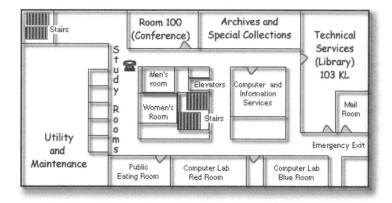

Second Floor

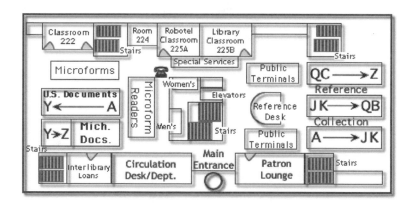

Third Floor

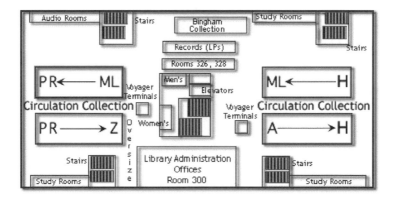

Fourth Floor

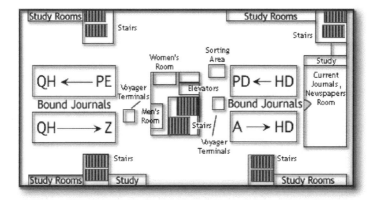

Writing Excellence Awards

Competition information

The Rhetoric Program holds an annual, special competition to encourage and support good writing. The following contest rules are available to students and faculty:

Each year, the department invites submission of high quality student writing for the Writing Excellence Awards competition. Papers are accepted in four categories: (1) Research papers submitted to RHT 160; (2) Any other type of paper submitted to RHT 150 or 160; (3) Papers submitted for credit in courses outside Rhetoric, Journalism, or English; and (4) papers submitted to advanced writing courses in Rhetoric, Journalism or English.

Prizes will include $100. for first place, $75. for second place, and $50. for third place in each category. You may submit your work in more than one category but only one paper per category. The judges will make only one award per student and reserve the right to allocate the awards in order to recognize the best writing in all categories.

Students should deliver papers to the Department of Rhetoric, Communication and Journalism, 316 Wilson Hall, no later than July 1. Please submit a typed or word processed paper that is free of technical errors. In order to facilitate an anonymous reading, *do not print your name or the name of your instructor on any page*, but make sure that you complete an entry form, including your own name and the name of your instructor with your paper. *Please note that the form must be signed by the Oakland University instructor in whose course the paper was accepted for credit.*

Winning essays from recent years can be found in the following pages.

◆

Award Winning Essays
Writing Excellence
Award Winners: 1999

The Straight Dope on Asthma:
As Told by an Asthmatic

Steve Dowdy

It is three in the morning and you are sound asleep. Suddenly you wake up choking with your mouth on fire. You jump out of bed and start coughing, but it is difficult because you are having trouble breathing. You are panicking, gasping for air. While you were sleeping, stomach acid crept up into your mouth because you were breathing so hard. Finally, you catch your breath, rinse your mouth with some water and down a handful of Tums to stop the burning in your throat. Before you go back to bed you take some medication to ease your breathing, but the medication makes you so hyperactive you will not be going back to bed. This seems like some sort of a nightmare; however, this is a description of a nighttime asthma attack I suffered from only a few weeks ago.

Asthma, as defined in the *Professional Guide to Diseases* is a:

Lung disease characterized by obstruction or narrowing of the airways, which are typically inflamed or hypersensitive to a variety of stimuli. It may resolve spontaneously or with treatment. Its symptoms range from mild wheezing to dyspnea ["A sense of difficulty breathing, often associated with heart or lung disease" (The New Book 407).] to life-threatening respiratory failure. Symptoms of bronchial airway obstruction may persist between acute episodes. (McMahon 333)

Having lived with asthma all my life, I can say that this is an accurate description of asthma (see appendix A for definitions of asthma and allergy related terms). Throughout the 23 years of my asthmatic life, I have tried many medications, treatments, and other things I call behavioral changes. While some have worked well, others have not. In recent years, many new drugs have been developed and the use of alternative medicine to treat asthma has risen. Because I continued to struggle with my symptoms, I wanted to learn more about these new treatments. During my investigation of the disease, I have learned much about these new cures and have even changed my own therapy consequently. Along the way to discovering my new medication regimen, I have tried numerous methods to suppress my symptoms, both medical and alternative. I have found that alternative medicines are great methods of treatment for some diseases. However, prescription medicine is the best choice for the long-term treatment of asthma.

Today asthma affects about 15 million people in the United States, 5 million of them children (Wasserman S-2). This is an astounding number and it is growing fast. "Asthma now afflicts at least one out of every 10 children in developed countries, a level that is twice what it was 2 decades ago" (Cookson 500). This does not come as much of a surprise to me because the diagnostic methods to distinguish asthma from other ailments have become more refined in the past few decades. The asthma patients were always there; they just were not diagnosed properly. Asthma is a nagging, persistent type of disease that requires constant attention to keep it under control. While prescription medicine is the most sought after remedy, over 165 million dollars were spent on homeopathic medicine, a type of alternative medicine, in 1994 alone (Garnett 1+). This definitely shows that Americans are interested in cures other than modern drug therapy.

Having been born with asthma, I have been on drugs ranging from Albuterol to Zafirleukast and although I have never gone out of my way to seek alternative therapies, I have inadvertently used them and will continue to use them because I believe they do have some positive effects. Do not misunderstand when I say I will continue to use alternative medicines. I do not use them exclusively; I use them only in conjunction with prescription drugs. Although I now make my own decisions about my health, this was not always the case. The story of my life with asthma and the variety of things my parents and I have done to treat it began when I was born. To find out what my asthma was like when I was an infant I consulted my mother (see appendix B for a complete transcript of the interview).

My mother, Sheila, told me that I was diagnosed as asthmatic when I was about two years old, but I was constantly sick before the diagnosis. The doctors told my parents to put a humidifier in my bedroom and to elevate the head end of my bed (Dowdy interview). These are two things which I still do to this day. These are not medical treatments or alternative medicines, but a modified behavior. Changing behavior in order to suppress symptoms is a substantial portion of an asthmatic life, as you shall read. My mother told me I constantly suffered from sinus problems when I was a baby (Dowdy interview). In the most recent study from the Johns Hopkins School of Medicine, it was shown that 95 percent of patients suffering from asthma also suffer from sinus allergies (Corren S-20). My doctor prescribed Benadryl for my sinus congestion (Dowdy interview). Today, I cannot take Benadryl without becoming comatose; I can only imagine what it did to me when I was a child.

I guess I had my first severe asthma attack when I was about two. I was at the babysitter's house when the attack took place. Everybody in the house smoked and they had cats, both of which I now know I am very allergic to (Dowdy interview). A recent study found that children from two months to five years old were twice as likely to suffer from asthma if their parents smoked twenty or more cigarettes a day ("If a Child's" F-3). I asked my mother if the doctor had ever told my father that he should not smoke in my presence and she said, "No, I guess they didn't know smoke was bad for you back then" (Dowdy interview). My response to that was, "And having a small fire dangling only inches from your face is always a safe thing to do!" I had to wait until I was five or six to be of allergy testing age (Dowdy interview). When I did finally get tested I found out that besides being allergic to cats and smoke, I was also allergic to chocolate, corn, mold, pollen (from grass and trees no less), and a whole list of things too long to print here.

To thwart my allergies the doctor decided to start me on immunotherapy; the dreaded allergy shots. This is when they take a small amount of refined allergens and inject them into the body. This has the effect of building immunity to the allergens, thus curbing the allergic reaction to them (Metcalfe S-14). I found this especially intriguing because one of the alternative medicines I mentioned earlier, homeopathy, is almost identical to this. Homeopathy works by taking an ultra low dose of a naturally occurring chemical compound, orally (Stohecker 273). The low dose is supposed to make the body immune to such compounds and the bizarre part of this treatment is the more dilute the dose of medicine, the stronger it becomes (274). Immunotherapy was mainstreamed long after homeopathy had already been discovered. Perhaps modern medicine has a few more things to learn from older alternative medicine practitioners. I did immunotherapy for only three years before I began having serious reactions to the injections. My arms would swell up and became very painful around the injection site. Upon asking my mother about this, she told me:

> I don't think the shots helped that much. I remember the nurse told you that you could punch her if the shot hurt and you let her have it. The doctor in New York wanted to make a serum just for you, instead of the broad spectrum one, but we moved and you quit getting the shots. I didn't see that it was doing you any good anyway. You still had all the same symptoms. You were constantly sick. (Dowdy interview)

Being a child, having a weak immune system, and trying to cope with asthma on a daily basis, I reluctantly had to stay at the hospital a couple times. My symptoms became so severe at one point that I had to stay for nearly a week. I had to get an IV so the doctors could keep a steady level of medication in me until I could breath on my own. I do not remember how old I was or what the medication was, but I did know what an IV was and that I did not want one. When it was time for me to get the IV, the nurse asked me if I was Steven. I replied, "No, I'm George." The nurse then got up and left the room. Nevertheless, my parents chased her down and asked her what happened. They all got a laugh out of it and I got the damn IV regardless. Older now, I know that the IV was in my best interest and the doctors did care about me, even though they had me tied down to the bed to keep me from pulling it out.

Hospitals are not a fun place to be when you are a kid. The food is bland, the beds are uncomfortable, and the only company you have is a bunch of sick, whiney kids. Missing school while in the hospital, my teachers would give my parents the homework I missed and sent it with them to the hospital. I do not know about you, but if you are sick enough to be in the hospital the last thing you need to worry about is homework! My aunt was just released from the hospital. She was on large doses of corticosteroids to stop inflammation in her lungs caused by asthma. My great grandfather died from an asthma attack while in his sleep, only a few days after being released from a hospital. While hospitals try to cure the symptoms of asthma, they do nothing for the person. The person lying in bed with the IV sticking out of their arm wonders if they are ever going to get better or how many times they will have to be back if they get worse. The only things that gave me comfort while I was in the hospital were my parents.

One type of alternative medicine my mother used to practice on me while I was in the hospital was massage. She would rub my feet and back while I lay in bed (Dowdy interview). Massage therapy, such as shiatsu, accupressure, and sports massage are calming techniques (Massage 90+). According to an article on massage therapy, "Some chronic ailments which are closely linked to stress, such as chronic headaches and asthma, may be improved by regular massage" (90+). I have found that if I am having asthma symptoms, rubbing my back lessens them. Asthma, because it is caused by constriction of the smooth muscles in the bronchi of the lungs, is probably reduced through massage due to its calming properties. It may allow the bronchi to relax, open up, and let more air out (Contrary to popular belief, during an asthma attack air has more of a problem getting out of the lungs than into them. This is due to the fact that human lungs work by a negative pressure system. That is, the lungs are designed to draw air into them, not push it out). My doctor advised my mother to repeatedly pound on my back with a cupped hand (Dowdy interview). I do not know if this was to help relax the bronchi, but it did help to relieve my congestion.

As for ingestion of any type of homemade remedies is concerned, our doctor told my parents to give me a mixture of whiskey, honey, and lemon juice as a cough suppressant (Dowdy interview). My parents did not have much money when I was small and making this was much more cost effective than paying for prescription medication. Moreover, it worked. Unlike some people who take these things and think they are something "natural," and not a medicine or chemical drug, I, having three years of university level chemistry, know they are drugs. Any herbal cure or mixture of these "natural" things should not be taken lightly. These cures contain chemical compounds just like modern medicines. For instance, a brochure for Asthma Clear from Ridgecrest Herbals states:

> Ephedrine, the active ingredient, takes care of the main system by restoring free breathing (compare this to similar relief provided by Primatene and asthma prescription drugs using a synthetic ingredient with side effects). In addition, drugs only work on symptoms and do nothing to restore the body to its normal, healthy state. As you can see from the description of

the other ingredients in Asthma Clear, they work on the cause of the asthma by restoring normal metabolic activities, reducing fluids, suppressing coughing and vomiting, etc.

Garbage! All a bunch of nonsense. The brochure states that ephedrine works by restoring free breathing. Is this not what Primatene and prescription medications are supposed to do? Does it make a difference that the chemical used in Primatene Mist (which is almost identical to ephedrine) was made in a lab? No, it is the same chemical whether synthesized by a plant or in a laboratory. The advertisement explains the side effects of using the synthetic drug, but nothing of the side effects of ephedrine. According to Dr. Pamela Gordon, a Detroit Medical Center cardiologist, ephedrine can cause hyperactive activity, loss of appetite, secretiveness, nausea, vomiting, dizziness, headaches, tumors, strokes, memory loss, and heart attacks (Bondi 6C+). Furthermore, herbal ephedrine is easy to obtain in large quantities and is the main ingredient in crystal methamphetamine manufacturing. The brochure goes on to state, "These statements have not been evaluated by the Food and Drug Administration. This product is not intended to diagnose, treat cure or prevent any disease" (Asthma Clear). If this product was not intended to treat, cure, or prevent asthma then why make it, and why take it?

I have taken ephedrine, but found that it has little effect on my breathing. Compared to my prescription medications it did nothing. Prescription asthma medications are powerful drugs that should only be used as directed. As with most herbal remedies, the amount of active ingredients per dose was not provided; the potency was not given either. This is scary because you usually do not know what you are getting. It's a guessing game.

Some herbal remedies are currently being tested as drugs. The latest herb to be examined is saw palmetto, an herb used for symptoms of prostate enlargement (Kirn 13). In the article about saw palmetto some information is given about what would happen if the FDA began checking the claims made by the manufacturer of the herbs (Kim 13). It states that if the FDA approves the Pharmaprint Company's saw palmetto it will cost 25% more than nontested brands (Kirn 13). If this holds true then it would be appropriate to suggest a price increase for all herbs. Herb manufacturers would want to get their products tested. Not only would it prove the validity of their claims of health improvement, but it would also increase the company's profits. That is, if you had your choice of cures, which would you choose? The FDA approved herbs or the non-approved herbs?

The first prescription medication that I was totally in control of taking was Albuterol in an inhalable form. I was eight years old when I started using Albuterol on a regular basis. Albuterol is also sold as Ventolin and Proventil, both of which are inhalable. The directions were take as needed, which meant during an asthma attack or before exercising. Because I was so young, I often did irresponsible acts such as leaving my inhaler in my gym locker or just plain losing it. I would not realize it was missing until it was time for me to go to bed or when I started having an attack. My father would often make a pilgrimage to the nearest all-night pharmacy to get another. This made him very upset, my being irresponsible, so I quickly learned how to keep track of my medication (Dowdy interview).

This was the only asthma medication that I had for many years. Even when I used the inhaler "as needed," I would continue to have symptoms, especially in the morning and in the spring or fall when the pollen and mold counts are highest. I just lived with the symptoms I had and continued to use the Albuterol inhaler at a rate of about 1.5 per month; the normal dosage was about one per month. I was eighteen when I noticed that my asthma seemed to be getting worse. I was involved in weightlifting at the time, which is anaerobic exercise; it does not bother my asthma as much as aerobic exercise does. While exercising, I found that my chest would become tight and congested. I consulted my physician and he gave me a prescription for Intal, another type of inhaler.

This bothered me. Having two types of inhalers to take around with me was very inconvenient. Furthermore, the Intal was not working as well as I thought it should be; it was expensive and left a bad taste in my mouth so I stopped taking it. It was not until I started to do research for the paper that I discovered why my asthma symptoms were always present. I discovered what Albuterol's purpose was after taking it for more than ten years. Albuterol is a quick-acting bronchi dilator. It works by relaxing the smooth muscles of the bronchi of the lungs during an asthma attack. This drug was created to provide short-term relief during asthma attacks; furthermore, it was not meant to be taken more than three times a week (Lichtenstein 39). For years, I was taking this drug, twice a day at the very least. Exactly as it had been prescribed by my doctors. No wonder it was not working anymore. Dr. Lichtenstein calls this the "rebound" effect; that is to say that when the short-term type medications are overused (or misused), the symptoms of asthma become worse (40). A few other types of quick acting, short term bronchodilators that I'm not familiar with are Theophylline, sold as Theo-Dur, Respid, Slo-Bid, Uniphyl, Slophyllin, Theo-24, and Theoluir (40).

Intal or Cromalyn Sodium is a long-term asthma controller (42). It was developed to treat occasional attacks caused by exercise, cold air, and allergy. Although the drug has few reported side effects, one of which is a bad taste in the mouth, it is safe and often prescribed for children (43). I found this drug of no value to me. Other drugs that are considered long acting are cortosteroids, nedocromil sodium, long acting beta agents, and leukotriene antagonists. The only other drug from this category I have experienced is the leukotriene antagonist.

After reading Dr. Lichtenstein's book, *Conversations about Asthma*, I made an appointment to see my physician. I told him what I had read about the overuse of Albuterol and how my asthma symptoms were still very persistent. He said, " In the past few years many new types of medications have been developed. Have you come across Accolate in your research?" (Bielak interview). I said, "Yes." Dr. Bielak then replied, "It's for patients of moderate to severe asthma. I want you to try it." Accolate or Zafirleukast, is by far the best medication that I have taken. I have been taking it for nearly three weeks and have used the Albuterol only once as a precautionary measure before exercise. Accolate, a small white pill, is to be taken twice a day on an empty stomach. Taking the medication on an empty stomach seems to be its only drawback. Sleeping is much easier now. I sleep through the entire night without worry of a nighttime attack. Dr. Lichtenstein also shares my opinion of prescription medication being the best defense against the symptoms of asthma (37).

The leukotreine antagonists are new drugs which were developed in 1996 and because they are so new not all of the physiological effects of their use have been discovered (Lichtenstein 45). Although a drug printout from the Rite Aid computer explains that the drug may cause headaches, nausea, or increased risk of infection, I have not experienced any such problems (Rite Aid). I recently discovered an advertisement for Combivent, an inhalable mixture of Albuterol and Atrovent. This drug works on two different areas of the lungs. The Atrovent works on the large airways of the lungs and Albuterol works on the small airways of the lungs, the bronchioles (Combivent). This was surprising to me because I did not know that different portions of the lung responded differently to the same drug.

Not all of my treatments were sought by ingesting chemicals, however. I did find relief from lower back pain through chiropractic medicine. When the chiropractor asked me if I had any chronic illnesses, I told him I had asthma. He told me that asthma could be cured by chiropractic manipulations of the spine. This is accomplished by adjusting the T-1 vertebrae (the first thoracic vertebrae) (Langone 99). The T-1 vertebrae, if displaced, could be the cause of asthma, cough, and pain in the lower arms and hands (99). The adjustments to my lower back did stop the pain and relieved the pinching of the nerve, but unfortunately, I found it to have no effect on my asthma. Chiropractor Dr. Edward G. Crealese said, "Chiropractors have seen kids who responded well to asthma treatment, and in fact we have many men who became chiropractors themselves simply because a chiropractor got them over their asthma" (108). I am happy to find chiropractic medicine working well for asthma, but I found no information on how it actually helped the victims.

During my investigations, I found many types of alternative medicines that seemed to have some credibility. Yoga claims to increase the stamina of the respiratory system, drain the lungs of fluid, restore energy to the entire body, and teach the lungs to relax (Mouro 67). In *Alternative Medicine*, yoga is portrayed as having "A beneficial effect on the respiratory system, with results ranging from lowered breathing rates and increased lung capacity to a diminishment of asthma attacks" (472). Osteopathy, which is very similar to chiropractic medicine, involves a diagnosis of musculoskeletal defects (Stohecker 405). According to Dr. Leon Chiatow, N.D., D.O., of London, a restriction of movement in the upper spiral region also effects the muscles that correspond to that area of the spine (405). He said, "A person with these restrictions may have a breathing problem, such as asthma, bronchitis, emphysema, or problems relating to a heart condition". He further claims that osteopathic manipulations will restore free movement to the spine, correct the muscles that function in breathing and prevent further illness (405).

Biofeedback is a method of training the autonomic body function with the aid of an electronic device (73). The devices used measure such things as heart rate, muscle tension, temperature, blood pressure, and brain activity. The machines give a visual or audible clue to whether these physiological variables are going up or down (University of California 6). According to *The University of California Berkley Wellness Letter* and *Alternative Medicine: The Definitive Guide*, biofeedback reduces the symptoms of asthma, insomnia, musculoskeletal disorders, hypertension, and headaches, with asthma responding especially well to the treatments. The articles go on to state that asthma sufferers learn how to increase inhalation volume, have reduced anxiety, and are generally more in control of their breathing.

Another alternative therapy that deserves mention is altitude chamber conditioning. Altitude chamber conditioning is the use of a hypobaric chamber to simulate the conditions of being at a high altitude (Altitude 1). I found this procedure on Dr. Allan R. Marshall's web site at *www.altitudechamber.com*. On the web site, Dr. Marshall's address was given to send for more information. When the information arrived I read it and found it interesting that Dr. Marshall gave the names of other doctors, who have articles on the Medline database, which is available at Oakland University in the Kresge Library. The articles explain the aspects of hypobaric therapy or "cellular calisthenics" as it is also referred to. The hypobaric conditioning is shown to increase chest size and red blood cell count and improve circulation (Altitude 1). Altitude therapy does make sense; it is the same technique employed by athletes to boost their performance. Athletes often train at high altitudes that contain less atmospheric oxygen than their bodies are accustomed too. By training at these thin air altitudes the athletes experience increased performance at normal, oxygen rich altitudes because their bodies have acquired mechanism to use oxygen more efficiently, thus shunting more oxygen into energy demanding tissues.

Earlier I mentioned that behaviors affected asthma. I know that behavior modifications are one of the best methods to control asthma, in conjunction with suitable prescription medications. The main changes I have made are mainly those in which I avoid stimuli that generate asthma symptoms. For me, these include avoiding my asthma triggers. Such triggers are exposure to cold weather, allergens, exercise, and nonallergens that include strong smelling substances or other chemicals which do not invoke an allergic reaction, but do provoke asthma. Behavior should also be considered a type of preventative medicine: A healthy habit. During my life with asthma, I have noticed that my daily routine has become suited to meet the needs of my disease. The modifications most likely started when I was young. My mother told me she would put me in a steamy bathroom to help relieve my congestion. She also told me that when I took my showers in the morning, I took a long time and allowed the water to become very hot (Dowdy interview). This was captivating because before I began taking Accolate I would often wake with congestion. The first thing I did was stand in an extremely hot shower; I realized I did this almost every morning. I guess that instead of the boy in the bubble, I was the boy in the bathtub! When I am sick, I do not consume any dairy products, phlegm products as I often call them. They just make more phlegm to choke on while you're trying to breathe. The avoidance of my triggers also includes not being able to go to a friend's house because of the cats or musty basement, or out to a club because of the smoke. It has even interfered with intimacy. Can you imagine telling your significant other they have to take a shower in order to continue the night's festivities because you are allergic to perfume?

Other habits I have formed include checking the weather channel to obtain information regarding the airborne allergy counts, avoiding nonsteroidal anti-inflammitories (aspirin, motrin, etc.), and keeping my bedroom very clean. However, the most important of these actions for me is keeping my room clean and knowing the allergen counts. Because my attacks were most prominent at night during sleep, clean bedding helped to rid my sleeping area of any allergens. *The Mayo Clinic Health Letter* suggests dustproofing mattresses and pillows with washable covers and washing sheets and pillow cases in hot water at least once a week to kill dust mites; furthermore, the bedding itself should not be constructed of down or foam, but tightly woven, nonporous materials such as Dacron (11). Knowing the pollen count is extremely important. For instance, if I wanted to do anything outdoors, I should wait until the allergen counts go down or I will become ill. During high pollen and mold spore counts I use my air conditioner, keep my windows closed, and if I must do something outdoors for any length of time, I wear a dust mask. According to the Mayo Clinic, central air conditioning is a great addition to the home of an asthmatic because a central air cleaner can be placed within the system to purify the air of the entire house (11). Placing cheesecloth over the register of the heater vents is another good method to trap airborne particles (Dowdy interview). Something I never thought of, probably because I wear glasses, is that when contacts are used during pollen season, pollen grains can become trapped under the contact lens and cause severe eye irritation (Mayo Clinic 11).

I have already mentioned that the head of my bed is elevated and that I use a humidifier, but did not explain why I did this. My bed is elevated about four inches by placing blocks under the legs of the headboard. This is because it helps to keep the acid in my stomach from oozing into my throat and mouth while I sleep. "Lung function normally fluctuates during a 24 hour cycle, it peaks at 4 p.m. to its low at 4 a.m. In asthma, this variation is more pronounced". This exact thing was giving me so many nighttime attacks. When I took my Albuterol inhaler before going to bed it wore off after only a few hours and then I would get sick; the drug was no longer working, my lung function was at its lowest peak and I would begin breathing heavy. This caused the nighttime attack and acid reflux. As far as the humidifier is concerned, I cannot give a definite answer. I do not have a humidifier in my room now, but I do have an aquarium. I replenish about two gallons of water per week so it must create some humidity. During my talk with Dr. Bielak, he told me that cold, dry air is one of the worst things for an asthmatic, but *The Mayo Clinic Health Letter* suggests keeping humidity levels low to reduce the growth of mold and dust mites. I suppose it is a trade off. When humidity levels are high you create a better environment for allergens to reproduce, and if they are too low the lungs may become inflamed. By keeping my room very clean, I have probably reduced the allergens' ability to multiply while reaping all the benefits of a higher humidity level.

For once in my life, I can say that my asthma is under control. I, however, can not say that it is gone because asthma never goes away completely. I have had many experiences with treatments; some good, some bad, but all have had an effect on how I now cope with being asthmatic. I am happy to admit that the research I have done for the paper has changed my life for the better, mostly by teaching me more about me. My asthma will always be lurking around the corner, but now I have an even bigger bag of tricks to help deal with it. My drug therapy will probably continue throughout the rest of my life, but I will continue to develop my so-called "healthy habits" and use alternative medicines for increased comfort. Everyone's asthma is different though, so what works well for me may not work well for someone else, but take into account my experiences and use them to your advantage. Take the time to read my Works Consulted list. The articles or books could be of help to you. After all, I did not use every bit of information I compiled in this work, but I did read all of it and it is very informative. Consult a specialist and develop a regimen that works for you, try some traditional medicines for further comfort, and above all do not be afraid to question your doctor about your medication. Take control of your asthma. It's like a breath of fresh air.

Works Consulted

"Acupuncture: Chinese Folk Medicine or Legitimate Medical Treatment." *Tufts University Health & Nutrition Letter* June 1998: 4–5.

"Allergy Glossary." *Discover* Mar. 1999: S–7.

A Shorter Intake of Breath 1 Jan. 1999 Online. Internet. Available *http://www.wt.com.au/~pkolb/but_theo.htm*

Apostolides, Marianne, Peele, Stanford. "It's No Longer All or Nothing." *Psychology Today* Sept./Oct. 1997: 32+.

Asthma Clear [Brochure] Ridgecrest Herbals information sheet. 1151 South Redwood Rd. Suite 106 Salt Lake City, UT 84104.

"Asthma." *Mayo Clinic Health Letter Feb.* 1996: 1–8.

"Asthma: The High Cost of Asthma Care." *Healthline* 17 (1998): 3–4.

Aziz, Imran, M.R.C.P., Lipworth, Brian J., M.D. "Exercise-induced Asthma." *The New England Journal of Medicine* 339, #24. Dec 10, 1998: 1783.

Berger, Abi. "Shallow Breaths Make Life a Wheeze." *New Scientist* Nov. 1995: 16.

Bielak, Daniel, D.O., family and sports medicine physician, Clarkston, MI. Personal Interveiw.

Blumenthol, Malcolm N., M.D., FAAAAI. "The Genes Behind the Disease." *Discover* Mar. 1999: S-20–S-24.

Bondi, Nicole. "Mom Wages War on Ephedrine." *Detroit News* 2 Dec. 1997: C-1+.

Busse, William W., M.D., FAAAAI. "New Approaches to the Treatment of Asthma." *Discover* Mar. 1999: S-16–S-19.

Chisholm, Patricia. "Healers or Quacks." *MacLean's* Sept. 1995: 34–39.

"Chronotherapeutics: Timely Treatments for Major Maladies." *Consumer Reports: On Health* May 1997: 52.

Combivent [Advertisement] *Family Practice News* 1 Oct. 1998: 42-42.

Cookson, William, O.C.M., Miriam F. Moffatt. "Alchemy for Asthma." *Nature Medicine: Vaccine Supplement* May 1998: 500–501.

Corren, Jonathan, M.D. "Connecting Hay Fever To Bronchial Asthma." *Discover* Mar. 1999: S-20–S-24.

Day, Michael. "Born Wheezers." *New Scientist* 11 Oct. 1997: 12.

Donahue, James G., Weiss, Scott T., Livingston, James M., Goetsch, Marcia A., Greineder, Dirk K. Et Al. "Inhaled Steroids and the Risk of Hospitalization for Asthma." *Journal of the American Medical Association* 19 March 1997, 277(11): 887–891.

Dowdy, Sheila. Mother, Ortonville, Mi. Personal Interview. 12 Mar. 1999.

Durso, Christopher. "Something Old, Something New." *The New Physician: American Medical Student Association* (47) Nov. 1998: 12–15.

"Exercise-induced Asthma." *Health News* 15 Aug. 1998: 10.

Fischer, Jessica. "Could This Mean the End of the Inhaler?" *Daily Mail (UK National Newspaper)* 16 May 1996. 1 Jan. 1999 Online. Internet. Availabe WWW: *http://www.wt.com.au/~pkolb/but_theo.htm*

Fireman, Philip, M.D., FAAAAI. "Deadly Morsels." *Discover* Mar. 1998: S-12.

Fireman, Philip, M.D., FAAAAI. "The Mechanisms of Allergic Inflammation." *Discover* Mar. 1999: S-25–S-26.

Fireman, Philip, M.D., FAAAAI. "The Most Common Allergy: Allergic Rhinitis." *Discover* Mar. 1998: S-13–S-14.

Fries, James F., M.D., Vickery, Donald M., M.D. *Take Care of Yourself.* Sixth ed. Reading, MA: Addison-Wesley Publishing Company, 1996: 118–121.

Frost, Bob. "Misery Has Company." *San Jose Mercury News* 13 Jul. 1997: 21+.

Garnett, Leah. "Homeopathy: Is Less Really More?" *Harvard Health Letter* May 1995: 1–3.

"Hypnosis: More Than a Suggestion." *Harvard Health Letter* Oct. 1997: 4–5.

"If a Child's Parents Smoke, Asthma Is More Likely." *Detroit Free Press* 3 Feb. 1998: F-3.

James, Dana. "Inside the OAM." *The New Physician: American Medical Student Association* Nov. 1998: 15–19.

Kirn, Timothy F. "Herbal Supplements Being Tested As Drugs." *Family Practice News* 15 Nov.: 13.

Langone, John. (1982). *Chiropractors: A Consumer's Guide.* Reading, Massachusetts: Addison–Wesley Publishing Company.

Lichtenstein, Lawrence M., M.D., Ph.D., Brown, Kathryn S. *Conversations about Asthma.* Baltimore, MD: Willaims & Wilkins: A Waverly Company, 1998.

Marshall, Allan R., Dr. *Altitude Chamber Conditioning.* [Pamphlet].

Marshall, Allan R., Dr. *Applied Kinesiology in Chiropractic Examination.* [Pamphlet] Systems DC: Pueblo, CO 1991.

Marshall, Allan R., Dr. *Introducing Altitude Chamber Conditioning.* On-line. Internet. Available WWW: *http://www.altitudechamber.com*

Marshall, Allan R., Dr. *References for Hypobaric Chamber Therapy and Related Subjects.* [Pamphlet].

Marshall, Allan R., Dr. *Structural Balance: The foundation of Health.* [Pamphlet] Systems DC: Pueblo, CO 1991.

Marshall, Allan R., Dr. *The "Total Person" Concept of Health.* [Pamphlet] Systems DC: Pueblo, CO 1993.

"Massage: The Healing Touch?" *Consumer Reports: On Health* Aug. 1996: 90-91.

Metcalfe, Dean D., M.D. "Allergy and Immunity." *Discover* Mar. 1998: S-8–S-10.

"Mind Over Body: Biofeedback." *University of California at Berkely Wellness Letter* 13 April 1997: 6–7.

McMahon, Edith, Fandek, Neal, Hodgson, Barbara, Norris, Crystal, eds. *Professional Guide to Diseases*. Fifth ed. Springhouse, Pa: Springhouse Corporation, 1995: 333–337.

Monro, Robin, Dr., Dr. H. R. Nagendra. (1990). *Yoga for Common Ailments*. New York: Simon & Schuster Inc.

Morris, William, Ed. et al. *The New Book of Knowledge*. [Dictionary Aa-Letterpress] Danbury, CT: Houghton Mifflin Company, 1980: 407.

Neimark, Jill. "On the Front Lines of Alternative Medicine." *Psychology Today* Jan./Feb. 1997: 52+.

Platts-Mills, Thomas A.E., M.D., Ph.D. "There's Something in the Air." *Discover* Mar. 1998: S-27–S-31.

Rachelefsky, Gary S. "The ABCs of Asthma." *Discover: The World of Science* Mar. 1998: S-1–S-4.

"Rite Aid Pharmacy Printout," Ortonville, MI. 14 Mar. 1999.

Roach-Monroe, Linda. "A Closer Look At Alternative Medicine." *Miami Herald* 23 May 1993: 1J+.

Stehlin, Isadora. "A Time to Heal: Chronotherapy Tunes in to Body's Rythems." *FDA Consumer* April 1997: 16–19.

Stohecker, James, ed. et al. *Alternative Medicine: The Definitive Guide*. Tiburon, CA: Future Medicine Publishing, Inc., 1997: 73–78, 272–278, 405–410, 469–481.

The Asthma Control Program From Glaxo Wellcome. [Pamphlet collection] Glaxo Wellcome Inc. Mar 1996.

"The Signs of Sinusitis." *Discover* Mar. 1998: S-16–S-18.

Theoretical Understanding Behind The Buteyko Technique 1 Jan 1999 Online. Internet. Available *http://www.wt.com.au/~pkolb/but_theo.htm*

"The Over-Medicated American." *Forcast* Dec. 1997: 6.

Wasserman, Stephen I., M.D. "*Introduction*." Discover Mar. 1999: S-2.

White, Nancy. "The Man With a 'Scientific Estate'." *The Journal Messenger* 6 Apr. 1985: A-1+.

Appendix A

Allergic reaction
An adverse immune response following repeated contact with otherwise harmless substances such as pollen, mold spores, animal dander, dust, food, cosmetics and drugs.

Allergy skin test
The injection of a small quantity of allergen into the skin to produce visible redness; used to identify which allergens are responsible for an individuals allergies.

Allergen

A foreign substance that leads to allergies by prompting an immune response.

Allergic rhinitis

Inflammation of the nasal mucous membranes due to an allergic response; sometimes called "hay fever."

Anaphylaxis

A medical emergency which involves an acute allergic reaction (one affecting the entire body). It occurs after exposure to an allergen to which a person was previously exposed.

Antibody

A protein (also called an immunoglobulin) that is manufactured by white blood cells called lymphocytes to neutralize an antigen or foreign protein as a part of the body's defense against infection and disease.

Antigen

A substance that triggers an immune response, resulting in the production of antibodies.

Antihistamines

A group of drugs that blocks the effects of histamine.

B – cells

White blood cells that are derived from bone marrow and are involved in the immune system's production of antibodies; they are also called B – lymphocytes.

Basophil

A type of white blood cell which circulates through the bloodstream.

Bronchiole

One of the thousand of tiny airways into which the larger airways, called bronchi, split, forming a tree-like network inside each lung.

Corticosteriod drugs

A group of anti-inflammatory drugs used for treating asthma, similar to natural hormones produced by the cortex of the adrenal glands.

Cytokines

A diverse group of protein molecules released by cells in response to activation or injury.

Dander

Small scales from animal skin; dander is a common allergen.

Eczema

An inflammation of the skin, usually causing itching and sometimes accompanied by crusting, scaling or blisters.

Eosinophil

A type of white blood cell important in modulating immune responses. High levels of these cells signal the presence of asthma or an ongoing allergic reaction.

Histamine

A group of chemical mediators of inflammation that stimulate the constriction of smooth muscle in the bronchioles.

Histamine-blocking agents

Drugs which impede the stimulation of cells by histamine. These agents act by interfering with the action of histamine rather than by preventing its secretion.

Hypersensitivity

A condition in a person previously exposed to a particular antigen, in which tissue damage results from an immune reaction to a further dose of the antigen.

Immunoglobulin E [IgE]

A class of antibody normally present in very low levels in humans but found in larger quantities in people with allergies and certain infections. Evidence suggests that it's the primary antibody responsible for the classic allergic reaction.

Leukotrienes

A group of chemical mediators of inflammation that stimulate the constriction of smooth muscle in the bronchioles

Lymphocytes

A group of white blood cells of crucial importance to immunity to specific antigens.

Mast cells

Cells that release and produce mediators of inflammation and are present in most body tissues but particularly numerous in connective tissues.

Mediators of Inflammation

Chemical substances that attract or activate other cells or chemicals in the immune response of allergy.

Monoclonal antibody

An antibody that is able to selectively recognize a single protein, peptide or chemical and interfere with their function.

Sensitization

Exposure to an antigen which results in IgE production and makes the patient susceptible to an allergic reaction.

Sinusitis

An inflammation of the membranes lining the air cells that surround the nose; often caused by bacterial or viral infection.

All definitions taken from the "'Allergy Glossary'" of the March 1999 *Discover* [special section] "The 1999 Asthma report" pages S-1 through S-26.

Appendix B

Personal interview with my mother, Sheila Dowdy. 12 March 1999

When was I first diagnosed as asthmatic?
> Sheila: Around one and a half to two years old. They couldn't run any test though because you were too young, you had to be a certain age. They did allergy testing in kindergarten or first grade.

So I was five or six ?
> Sheila: Yes, before you were diagnosed I was constantly in the Dr.'s office. We elevated your crib and had a humidifier in your room. You constantly had sinus problems. You took a lot of Benadryl when you were small. You picked your nose a lot because it was always plugged up.
>
> When you were two you had your first asthma attack at the babysitters. They all smoked and had cats. You got really sick.
>
> You started on allergy shots every week, for at least three years. I don't think they helped much though, but your food allergies never bothered you that much.

Did you ever consider seeking any alternative medicines for me?
> Sheila: No, I never did. I never thought it would help.

What was the whiskey, honey, and lemon juice concoction I used to take?
> Sheila: That was for croup cough, it was a cough suppressant. The Dr. told us to make. It worked really good.

When I was young, how did asthma affect my social life?
> Sheila: We had you stay inside when the leaves were being burned, and when dad mowed the lawn. Also, when the road was too dusty. We made you wear a mask a few times, but you got bent

out of shape. You also have to remember that nobody said that cigarette smoke was bad and your father had always smoked in the house.

You were around one and a half or two when I found out you were very bad with cats. We thought your eyeballs popped out they looked so bad! You weren't a crybaby though, you were very content.

We put you in the bathroom with the hot shower running and taking you outside seemed to help sometimes, but sometimes it didn't.

I know you said you had never sought alternative therapies, but you did used to rub my feet when I was sick. Did it seem to help my symptoms?

Sheila: I did massage your feet a lot and I pounded on your back when you were congested. I thought it made you feel better when you were sick.

Massage causes relaxation of the muscles and asthma is caused by muscle spasms. Do you think the relaxation helped relax my spasms?

Sheila: I think that's what it was. When you were in the hospital, you always wanted me to do your feet. You were ornery in the hospital.

Did the Dr. suggest any behavioral changes that would help me?

Sheila: No, you never really did anything to make yourself sick, it was just the environment, I guess. The Dr. told us to keep you playing water sports though.

You asked me to pound on your back a lot. I cupped my hand and beat on your back to help loosen the phlegm. You did like it.

99 percent of the time you got sick at nighttime. You would cope with it all day long and then at night you'd say, "Mom, dad, take me to the hospital." You would wait until everything closed before you told us you needed an inhaler, because you lost it or left it at school.

Do you think the overall health of the family has improved since people started smoking outside?

Sheila: That's a hard one. Yours has, but nobody else is really allergic to smoke. I could tell a big difference in you though. I could tell a big difference when we got the new furnace too. The wood burning all the time probably made you sick a lot more. My sinuses hardly ever bother me with the humidity in the house.

When did I start on the inhaler medication?

Sheila: I want to say about . . . I thought you were too young, but I think you were seven.

Did I ever have side effects from the medications?

Sheila: No, and I can't remember. I think you only took it before you went to bed. Then they put you on pills for a while.

Do you know what the pill was?

Sheila: No. I remember when you were getting your allergy shot. The nurse said, "You could punch her if it hurt." You let her have it! Your shots started hurting you though and your arms would swell up real big. You would get a big welt around the shot and they cut back your medicine.

In New York the Dr. wanted to make a serum just for you instead of the broad spectrum one they were giving you. We moved and you quit getting the shots. I didn't see that it was doing you any good anyway. You still had the same symptoms. You were constantly sick anyhow.

When we lived up north, you were very sick. I don't think the cows bothered you, but the wood stove, old house, and being in the barns did. It really bothered you when we cut the hay. I don't think you were sick too much with asthma in New York, but you were deathly ill with the chicken pox. You always had a snotty nose though.

One day when it was very cold out you came in from playing and you said you needed your inhaler.

How many times was I hospitalized as a child?

Sheila: Two times. Once for the flu and the second time was for asthma. They were giving you IV medication.

How many times did I have to go the ER?

Sheila: Maybe six or seven times, but we were always at the doctors. You were constantly sick. They would give you the adrenaline shots at the doctor's office and you would be wired. Kicking your legs like crazy. We had to stay so they could take your pulse and blood pressure. Usually you would be wired for awhile, then you would fall right asleep.

Even with all of your problems, you never had pneumonia.

Do you think that's because you kept such a close eye on me?

Sheila: Yes, I really do. We never gave you anything over the counter. We gave you Triaminic, but the Dr. told us to. I was afraid to give you anything over the counter because everything says do not take if you have asthma. I do remember the Dr. telling me to give you flat pop. Yeah, that's when you had stomach aches.

The Dr. told me to give you lots of fluids and slowly start you on solid foods. When you came home from the hospital with the flu. You demanded hot dogs. You ate two of them and it didn't seem to hurt you.

How do you think being asthmatic as a child has affected me as an adult?

Sheila: You don't get excited when you get sick. It's like no big deal. Shots didn't bother you. Neither did the Dr.'s office. Totally opposite of your sister. I think you've grown to respect your body a lot more. You know if you do something your gonna get sick, so you don't do it. Attitude wise you haven't changed since you were three. You were a shit. You would get frustrated when things didn't go your way. You got violent.

Did I ever complain about my medication?

Sheila: I don't remember you ever complaining about it, until you got older. When you were younger, you would stay in the shower, hot, until the hot water ran out. I think it makes you feel better in the morning because your asthma bothered you so much at night. You still take long showers.

Can you remember anything else you used to do to help my asthma?

Sheila: I used to put cheesecloth over the air vents because the furnace didn't have a filter. You used to get sick in the fall when it got cold and the furnace kicked on for the first time since the last winter. Blowing all the dust around.

Bearing Witness to the Holocaust

Seth Schindler

Late August is one of northern Germany's best months. When I visited there in the summer of 1997, the heat was intense but not unbearable. The winding streets were lined with adorable little homes, and sounds of children filled the air. This picturesque little neighborhood in Germany's Sachsen-Anhalt province could have easily been mistaken for the set of *The Sound of Music*. On the other side of the street, however, rose a fifteen foot cement wall. This was my first clue that we had arrived at Sachsenhausen Concentration Camp.

For as long as I can remember I've been fascinated by history. Many people cringe when they hear the word, but for me it's an infinitely interesting subject. I wanted to visit a concentration camp more that anything else when I was in Germany, for reasons I cannot explain. The Holocaust is so fascinating because people always imagine themselves as being there, as the victims and as the Nazis. It's impossible to comprehend being treated as subhuman or killing thousands of strangers, but everyone tries, at least subconsciously. Due to my personal fascination with the Holocaust I had read extensively on the subject before going to Germany. This made my visit to Sachsenhausen come to life because I could put everything into historical context.

My best friend hosted an exchange student sophomore year in high school. It took us about a month to knock down the language barrier, but after that Chriss was accepted into our group of friends. He brought a certain type of recklessness and humor to our group, and we became very close. It was hard to see him go, and it didn't really set in that he had left until about a week after he was gone. We stayed in touch however, and I flew to Berlin to see him the summer before my senior year. World War II was always a difficult subject for us to discuss. Although Chriss is vehemently anti-Hitler, both of his grandfathers fought against the Russians in the German army. I always sensed that this burdened him, and he never felt comfortable talking about anything which concerned the war. For this reason it was difficult to persuade him to take me to Sachsenhausen. He wanted to show me the Brandenburg Gate and Potsdamer Platz, symbols of Germany's greatness, but I was more interested in Germany's lowest point.

We walked into a forest on a cobblestone path and followed the ominous wall. Other people were going in the same direction as we were but no one spoke. Some people were crying, and others just showed solemn expressions of guilt or sorrow. One middle aged woman dressed in black was sobbing uncontrollably. The forest thinned and we stepped into a large courtyard dominated by a symmetrical white building on the far side. It rose like a tumor out of the cobblestone and seemed to block out the sun. Following the masses who came before us, we slowly walked toward an iron gate which hung under the villainous white building. It was the original gate, and the metal bars still spelled the words "Arbeit Macht Frei" or "Work will make you free." This sick Nazi joke was their way of saying "Welcome to Sachsenhausen Concentration Camp."

Tall guard towers are the first thing which will catch any visitor's eye. They spring out of the cement wall which circles the camp. Mangled clumps of rusty barbed wire paralleled the impassable wall. Sachsenhausen had been one of the main concentration camps during World War II from which Hitler and his cronies mercilessly attempted to destroy European Jewry. When it was obvious the Russians would not be stopped, the SS tried to demolish Sachsenhausen, thus eliminating evidence of their crimes. For this reason a large memorial tower dominates the parade grounds rather than rows of barracks. Only two barracks survived the carnage and they now serve as museums. A plaque commemorates the ground where the gallows once stood, but for the most part the inside of the camp is just a barren field.

There was plenty more to see in Sachsenhausen than I initially thought. We hiked across the immense field to the back of the camp. Large wooden doors were propped open to allow visitors into the former marshaling area where thousands passed before being executed. The crematorium and gas chambers were blown up in the final days of the war, so that all that remains is the foundation. We walked down a road large enough for two carriages to pass. Once at the bottom, we were surrounded by earth. Logs were stacked on one side of the earthen mound about twenty feet tall. The sun couldn't penetrate into the bottom of the pit, but weeds managed to cover the three bare sides. This was the heart of the Sachsenhausen killing machine. A firing squad continuously killed prisoners. Prisoners walked to their death down the two-cart path past their friends' and families' dead bodies which were being wheeled to the crematorium in the left lane.

The other side of the camp saw just as much brutality, but the Nazis were secretive about it. Instead of large wooden doors, a small metal one broke the monotonous pattern of the white wall. If you passed through this door while the camp was in operation, you could expect torture and eventually death. But now all you see are the remnants of a secret Gestapo prison which houses a museum. Worn out instruments of torture now serve as displays. Half of it lies in charred ruins due to a fire set by right wing extremists in 1995 during the ceremony commemorating the 50th anniversary of liberation. The destroyed building now serves as a reminder to visitors of the controversy that remains. A sign explains in many languages what happened, and honors those who work to preserve history. This shows all too clearly that the Holocaust is not yet over. Of course gas chambers no longer bellow ashes, and railroads no longer carry people to their death in cattle cars. Today's Holocaust is being waged in people's minds. History is the new victim. Some extremists claim the Holocaust never happened, and revisionist historians are apathetic toward the Holocaust. They make excuses for the German people. Of course ninety percent of the Germans didn't directly aid the Holocaust. They minded their business across the street from tall white walls all over the Fatherland.

Although guard towers are empty and the executions have ceased, my visit to Sachsenhausen was very intense. After two hours of bearing witness I was physically and emotionally drained. The camp was paradoxically peaceful yet imcomparably stressful. I had a throbbing headache. I was very hungry and my legs had no bounce left in them. We again plodded past the crematorium, Gestapo prison, and barracks. We passed through the gates under the symmetrical white building into the tranquillity of the forest. The children were still playing when we got to the neighborhood. We ate at McDonald's and I took some aspirin. I soon felt rejuvenated. But what if I wasn't allowed to leave? The prisoners couldn't decide to go to McDonald's because they were hungry. If a prisoner decided they were too hungry to continue working the only way out was death. Sachsenhausen made the Holocaust come alive for me. No longer was it ink on paper listing statistics which I could never comprehend. It was now a living, breathing, sweating, and bleeding thing. I now see real people when I imagine the Holocaust. I see innocent people: wives, brothers, fathers and grandparents. People that you know just disappeared: the postman, your teacher, your classmates, and possibly even you. I'm ashamed to say it but I thanked God it wasn't me trapped there, for I would have been one of those emaciated bald prisoners with haunting stares had I passed under the symmetrical white building 60 years earlier.

The Flipside of Technology

B. Joshua Simon

The New Yorker, an upscale weekly literary magazine, contains many cartoons that satirize the fast-paced New York lifestyle. On page 90 of the January 4th, 1999 Edition one finds such a cartoon. The cartoon depicts a man forcefully seated in a chair while reading a book. The seated man is wearing plain shorts and a T-shirt, tennis shoes and socks. His glazed facial expression resembles that of a person in a catatonic state. Above the drawing appears the caption, "NORDIC TRAK READING MACHINE,"—an innovative new machine designed to address the problems a modern technophile might encounter in trying to sit down and relax with a book. This machine features two new state-of-the-art items including: a reading lamp to counter excuses like "I don't have good reading light" and an electronic arm which "Holds book and turns pages at whatever speed you set." In addition, several physical restraining devices ensure that the man will remain seated long enough to spend quality time reading his book. These include straps for the chest, arms, and legs, a helmet, and earflaps, with each device serving a specialized purpose as described in the text of the cartoon. The helmet forces the head to remain in the correct reading position; earflaps mute any distracting sounds; chest, arm, and leg straps prevent any telephone calls, sudden urges to grab the remote control or get up for a snack.

The overall visual impact of the cartoon is stunning. In the center of the frame, the man sits inside the machine. Coupled with the physical restraining devices, the electronic arm holds the book directly in front of the man's eyes while the oversize reading lamp looms above, thus adding to his, and our, feeling of entrapment. Literally surrounded by this gigantic machine, the man sits wide-eyed staring at the text in front of him. In an outer circle encompassing the entire machine, written captions advertise its appealing features (the physical restraints as well as the technological advances incorporated in the design). The visual arrangement of these captions in a tight circle contributes greatly to the feeling of being consumed by the machine.

Upon examining this cartoon, several questions arise about the value of technological advancement. First, what type of consumer would purchase a product such as this machine? Obviously some type of masochist! Yet, as the author suggests, perhaps this is the very thing Americans do through continual desire of the most recent technology while simultaneously discarding older, time-tested hobbies such as

[margin note: Rhetorical question? Could be Thesis?]

reading. On the forefront of the next millenium, Americans find themselves in an ever changing, constantly "advancing" environment. Is this due in part to the desire to be the biggest, fastest, strongest and best? How ironic it all seems that the personal rights and freedoms instilled in each American through centuries of democracy have driven us to seek machines designed to restrain that very freedom. The cartoon implies that without the necessary physical restraint, modern man does not possess enough self-control to sit down and relax with a book. Is our society so enraptured with the notion of instant gratification that we need a machine to force us down to read? The cartoon suggests that people are too consumed by vending-machine nutrition, cellular telephones and remote control to sit down and casually focus on the contents of a book. The cartoonist assures us that if technology continues to proceed without respect for the past, then mankind will become a total zombie, completely devoid of all humanity. After eliminating all impulses, perhaps this zombie-like personality would be all that remained.

I believe the cartoon makes fun of the current revolution in fitness machines as well. It uses the current trend in home fitness equipment to illustrate the overall need in America for bigger, faster, and stronger. The name given to the cartoon, "NORDIC TRAK READING MACHINE," places a recognizable title, "NORDIC TRACK™," upon a new intervention. This title satirizes the trendy, name brand of "NORDIC TRACK™" by juxtaposing it with a ridiculous concept such as a reading machine. However, when first introduced in America, people considered the "NORDIC TRACK™" machine too different from the norms in current fitness technology to succeed in the industry. Today many people spend more time working out than reading. By combining the machine necessary for a total body workout with the open book, the cartoon forces one to examine the amount of time spent reading on a daily basis. As a society we spend a considerable amount of time and money on fitness equipment to take care of the body, yet how often do we make a workout for the mind a top priority? *[margin note: Just write it out!]*

[margin note: Assumes we know what a Nordic Track is]

The cartoon raises the issue of self-control, or lack thereof, in technologically advanced societies. Upon entering the machine, the man becomes impervious to distracting sounds. Are we to assume that, without the aid of a machine, every sound that enters our consciousness might distract from the current task at hand? Perhaps as the cartoon implies, the overwhelming amount of information accessible in 1999 causes one to lost interest quickly or easily become distracted. With so much information now available literally at our fingertips, attention spans have diminished, thus resulting in frequent distraction, confusion, and overall lack of focus.

The machine declares itself a technology advancement, but one of the major intentions of this technology is to block the man from using other technology. Without the use of his hands, the man sits restrained from any movement towards his cellular telephone or remote control. Here, again, the cartoonist forces one to examine the benefits of such technology.

Admittedly, technology has brought a great deal of benefit to American society, but one must recall the initial intention of technological progress: to help the common good of society. Examination of this farcical cartoon allows one to explore the various drawbacks inherent in technology advancement. These include: a lack of respect for the technology of past generations; the loss of self-control, focus, and motivation as we continue to rely more heavily upon machines; the irony of designing a machine with the direct purpose of restraining us from using other forms of technology. Only through thorough examination of current, as well as past, forms of technology may we truly continue to "advance" as humans.

tied in with the rest
State the point of the paper or the paper

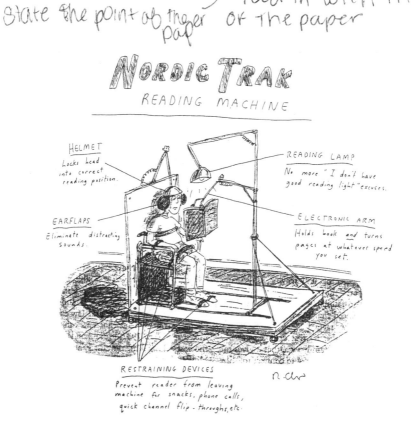

Buy Me Some Peanuts and Cracker Jack

by Kathleen I. Bethell

It is a well-known fact that a spectator in the stands at the ballpark has need of frequent refreshment. This is especially true on hot days, when the mid-summer sun is at full strength and the shirtless bleacher bums are as crisply roasted as hot dogs turning on a grill. It stands to reason, therefore, that few human beings are welcomed with as much enthusiasm as the drinks vendors at a baseball game. "Beer here!" shouts the patron saint of the thirsty, "Getchyer ice cold beer!" The beer is usually on the tepid side of lukewarm, but a sip of it has power to restore failing vocal chords. For those tireless fans whose destiny calls them to jeer loudly each time an opposing player steps up to the plate, no price is too high for this voice-preserving tonic. "Beer here! Getchyer ice cold beer!"

The beer man, of course, is not a one-man entertainment. An entire chorus of vendors serenades the thirsting throng. Their voices blend in a euphonious hymn of promise—refreshment is at hand! The notes of an aria rise above the chorus to entreat the reluctant flock: "Colacolacola! Co-la, co-la!" To my ear, the plangent notes of this vendor's song sound like the call of the black-capped chickadee, and is just as insistent. A baritone sings out in counterpoint, "Pro-o-o -gram! Fourdollarsfora Pr-o-o -gram!" Some tenors join in, selling popcorn and cotton candy. "Hot dogs—Get 'em while they're hot!"—are peddled in a rhythmic, raspy challenge. To me, these voices sing songs of salvation, and are as much a part of baseball as the game itself. Often on a hot summer evening at Tiger Stadium, I have heard a vendor's voice calling to me over the tumult of the crowd, and known that comfort was at hand. If I hungered, they fed me; if I thirsted, they gave me drink—for a few dollars or so. That the vendors would always be there to succor the needy was more than a matter of faith; it was a certainty.

This past summer, however, there came a day when the vendors' voices were all but silenced. It was a day that tried my faith sorely. The crisis came shortly after 7:05 on a Thursday evening, during an interleague baseball game between the Detroit Tigers and the Chicago Cubs. That evening, June 25, 1998, I had a revelation. I learned, to my great distress, that, although some things may be eternal, ballpark vendors are not. They are ephemeral and evanescent, perhaps even illusory. They can disappear. In consequence, I am no longer beguiled into complacence by their song, for I know that it, like the vendors, can evaporate in the heat of a summer day.

The summer of 1998 was to be my baseball summer, the summer in which I proposed to both reacquaint myself with the game and to get to know the Detroit Tigers as my home team. I'd lost track of baseball five years earlier, back in 1993, when my husband was transferred from Madison, Wisconsin to the Detroit area, and we had to relocate our family. Tickets for superb seats at Tigers' home games became available for our occasional use, but I felt no desire to make use of them. I didn't care how good those seats were, because the Tigers were not my team. The Milwaukee Brewers were my home team, and County Stadium was my ballpark. I wasn't about to trade them for another team in an unknown stadium in an unfamiliar, scary-looking city. Before our move to Detroit, I had developed a comfortable habit of listening to Bob Uecker's radio broadcasts of the Brewers' games. Although we had enjoyed numerous family outings to the ballpark to see the games in person, we lived too far away to make the trip to Milwaukee a habit. So it was up to the radio and Bob Uecker to keep me tuned in regularly to a vicarious ballpark experience. Uke did not let me down. He was an extension of my own senses, and he was at his best when he'd let his attention wander between plays, the way my own so often did, to fill me in on all those other details that make a ball game memorable. He'd talk of beach balls and balloons being batted from section to section in the stands, of fans trying to get the crowd to do "the wave," of the sunlight glinting off the bald head of the first base coach, and of the tireless efforts of the bat boy to get clean baseballs to the umpire when a spitballer was pitching. He'd describe the colors of the sunset, the autumnal chill in the air, and the heady aroma of a burning automobile wafting in from the parking lot—this latter phenomenon caused by a careless tailgate picnicker who'd stowed his barbecue grill in the trunk of his car at game time with the hot coals still in it. Best of all were Uke's culinary reviews, in which he'd sample and report on the relative merits of the vendors' wares at whichever ballpark the Brewers were visiting. I don't think he ever met a ballpark snack he didn't like, but he'd always qualify his praise, giving top marks only to his home park's cuisine. The Kowalski sausage served at Tiger Stadium, for example, was admired, but it could never stand up to the virtues of Milwaukee's sizzling Johnsonville bratwurst smothered in Secret Stadium Sauce.

I liked Uke's voice and his wry sense of humor. After the move, I found I couldn't bear to listen to baseball games announced by other voices. A while later, all the major league players went on strike, and the Brewers changed leagues, and the players I knew so well got traded or got old and quit the game. In a sulk, I quit paying attention to baseball altogether—until last summer, which is when I resolved to fall in love again.

As is usual in matters of the heart, it was jealousy that made me change my mind about baseball. In the years before he left for college, my son, Nathan, became a Tigers fan. It was not the time he spent at Tiger Stadium that piqued me, but rather his devotion to the very thing that I had spurned. I was like a jealous lover; I wanted baseball back for my own, even though it wore a Tigers uniform. Fortunately for everyone's sake, baseball is generous with its affections. The more people who love the game, the more beautiful it becomes. To be completely honest, in these past few years, the Detroit Tigers have not been beautiful. They've been more of an ugly duckling than a winsome and graceful swan. It is hard to love a team that battles valiantly for last place, but for some reason Nathan does love them. Even more, I think, he loves the old stadium at the corner of Michigan and Trumbull Avenues, the grand old park still radiant with past glories even in these, its last, declining years.

So, in the summers of his high school years, before he headed off for college, Nathan and his buddies drove out to Tiger Stadium every time they could scrape up the money for a ticket. I asked once how the boys managed to afford refreshments on their limited student incomes, and was advised on the nature of the economic incentives offered to fans by awful teams desperate for an audience. The Detroit Tigers these past few years are a truly awful team, so the incentives to attend have become impressive. Just eight dollars will buy a ticket, a hot dog, and a paper cup full of warm Pepsi. If you sit out in the center field bleachers, the ticket will cost only four dollars. Out there, on those torrid days when only a few fans show up and business is slow, you might be lucky enough to experience what the stadium management calls Malt Cup Madness. Ice cream vendors will suddenly converge on the bleacher section and begin throwing their stock into the crowd. A small riot ensues, during which the quickest and most agile fans can gather in a harvest of frozen malt cups and a complement of tiny wooden paddles with which to eat the rapidly thawing mess. My son reports that his record take for one such melee was eight malt cups, which spared him the necessity of purchasing any other nourishment that day.

Despite such enticements, I did not get around to rekindling my romance with baseball until this past summer, when Nathan returned home from his first year at college. He had been getting his education in another state, a remote place that saw fit to televise only Cubs and White Sox games. Still, he remained a loyal Tigers fan, and he planned to make more than a few pilgrimages to Tiger Stadium during his summer at home. Unfortunately, most of his friends remained away at their various schools, and did not returned to Detroit. Nathan was disappointed, of course, but I saw my opportunity. I pointed out that baseball games are not much fun when viewed alone, and I quickly volunteered to accompany him to whatever ball games he wanted to attend.

I have painted myself as the jealous lover of a spurned sport, but that is not entirely a true portrait. Another, more primal, urge also impelled me to reacquaint myself with baseball in the summer of 1998. This was a sort of maternal stickiness, a tenacious but doomed love that didn't want to let go of my son. I had more than survived the empty nest of the previous winter; I believed I had sailed through my first childless school year with admirable poise and élan. So, when Nathan finally did return home after that first year away, I was astonished to discover how much I wanted simply to spend time with him.

I did not exactly grovel for the privilege of accompanying him to the ballpark, but I admit that I did stoop to a sort of benign coercion. I offered to open my wallet and pay for parking and refreshments. I also volunteered to buy our tickets. I did, however, assign him one task. His job was to select our seats, since he was the more familiar with the layout of the ballpark. I am grateful that he allowed me to come along with him. And I must confess that I thoroughly enjoyed the comforts of watching the games from our thoughtfully chosen box seats.

It was a sweltering ninety-eight degrees on the afternoon of the first ball game we saw together. The forecast was for little decrease in temperature during the course of the evening; even after sundown, we would continue to bake. I knew that Tiger Stadium, set amidst the concrete of the city, would be oppressive by game time that night. Still, we had made our plans; Nathan and I were going to the ballpark, right after Nathan finished work. I packed up a change of clothes for him so he could enjoy the game in what comfort he could. I brought shorts, T-shirt, sunglasses, and his long-billed, triple-A team baseball cap with the Quad City River Bandits logo on front. I brought ice water to drink on the way to the stadium in case we were stuck in heavy traffic too long. I did not, however, pack refreshments for the game; that sort of thing is contraband at the ballpark. Refreshments are for the vendors to provide.

In the car, we talked about the evening's game, an inter-league contest against the Chicago Cubs. I don't remember who the Tigers were planning to pitch that night, but Nathan was eager to get a look at the Cubs' pitcher, a promising kid named Kerry Wood. Another Cubs attraction was some guy who had suddenly begun hitting an incredible number of home runs at the end of May, and was out-doing himself again this month, in June. If we were lucky, Nathan told me, we might even get to see him break the record for most home runs in a single month. Nathan talked so much about the Cubs' line-up, I began to suspect that his allegiance to the Tigers had been compromised while he was away at school. He assured me that, since the Cubs and the Tigers played in different leagues, it was okay to like them both.

I was happy to receive this intelligence, since I was suffering from a mild case of divided loyalties myself. I was still resolved to ally myself with the Detroit Tigers, but I knew I was going to have trouble with this particular game. I had been busy, with one thing and another, and I still had not found time to learn the Tigers' line-up. I knew only one player's name, but didn't know if he was scheduled to play that day. I wasn't even entirely sure what our uniforms looked like. Furthermore, I am a native Chicagoan. My memories of childhood include a sound-track on which the late Harry Carey and Jack Brickhouse of WGN provide backup vocals on the summertime tracks. In the years before I went to Wisconsin, baseball was always played in the Friendly Confines of Wrigley Field by the eternally hopeful (and perpetually disappointed) Chicago Cubs. Small wonder that Chicago's uniforms looked more familiar to me in Tiger Stadium than the home-game whites the Tigers were wearing. Old habit was resurrected at the sight of Cubbie Blue, and I found myself cheering the wrong team at critical moments during the game. Holy Cow! Hey! Hey! My attention slipped, and the Cubs received my accolades when, by rights, I should have been groaning in sympathy with the Tigers. Not that they needed my sympathy; the Tigers went on to win that game. They even swept the series against the Cubs.

My attention slipped a lot in the furnace-like heat of that late June evening at Tiger Stadium. The ballpark, much to our delight, was overflowing with an abundance of fans. They were Chicago fans, for the most part, but it was glorious to be part of a crowd that roared and cheered and delighted in the intricacies of the game being played out on the grassy field under a darkening sky. Subsequent games seemed silent and lonely after the tumult of the Cubs series. The crowd had materialized, it seems, without warning, spilling out of buses and vans, gathering in swarms of happy anticipation around the ticket booths at every gate. It was a spontaneous celebration of baseball that converged upon Tiger Stadium that Thursday night, and it caught the management completely by surprise. Cubs fans, I've since learned, will travel anywhere to see their ball club play. Tickets to games at Wrigley Field are next to impossible to obtain, so the fans settle for the next best thing. They buy tickets for the Cubs' away games, and fill the stands at ballparks throughout the midwest. In 1998, the Cubs looked good, and by the end of May, they had one player that everybody wanted to see. And so the people came.

The Detroit Tigers, on the other hand, are not a hot ticket, not by a long shot. Their stadium is a serene backwater nowadays, where a few aficionados (die hards, some call them) gather to reminisce about the glory days when Al Kaline ruled right field, or when Lou Whitaker at second and Alan Trammell at short combined in a near-impenetrable defense against all comers. But that was awhile ago; these days, tickets at Tiger Stadium are not hard to come by. If you want to see a game, just show up. You can buy your tickets at the gate; there's no need to order them ahead of time. The Cubs fans, it seems, knew all about this.

The Chicago Cubs are a National League ball club; the Detroit Tigers are an American League affiliate, and, until inter-league games were introduced, the Cubs had never before been guests at Tiger Stadium. So, to be fair, perhaps the Tigers' management hadn't heard about the Cubs' magnetic ability to attract a crowd. Perhaps they dismissed such rumors as exaggerated. It had been so long, after all, since the Tigers had come even close to filling the stadium at the corner of Michigan and Trumbull. Perhaps I am making excuses for the inexcusable. But then, what excuse can there be for nearly killing a sellout crowd at your own ballpark?

The air was close and heavy at game time on June 25th, even after the sun went down. Nathan and I were but two drops of perspiration in a sea of sweating thousands who converged on Tiger Stadium that night. Still, we were jubilant in the jostling crowd that thronged the sidewalks and overflowed onto the streets. We were eager as we surged like cattle through the turnstiles, up the ramps, and into the tunnels beneath the stands. We were confident, as we emerged into the open air of the ballpark and took our seats. It was hot, sweltering hot, and we were sitting among strangers, uncomfortably near to each other. In the good seats, the seats that offered the best views of the field, the seats for which we'd all clamored, the crowd sat shoulder-to-shoulder. Still, we were confident. We were confident that our discomfort would subside, that a breeze would kick up, that vendors would soon visit our section and bring us sweet liquids to cool our overheated bodies and moisten our parched throats.

A faint zephyr did skip through toward the end of the ball game, but it did little to cool us. I don't put much faith in weather. It's too capricious. The vendors are another matter. When they didn't show up that night, my faith in them was badly shaken.

William Zinsser once described the purgatory that a person awaiting jury duty endures. He sits alone and silent in a crowd of solitary, silent strangers with nothing to contemplate except the stupefying fact of waiting. For Zinsser the waiting was always futile. He was never called to be a juror, although he waited patiently every two years as instructed. I waited patiently, too, last June at Tiger Stadium when the Cubs came to town. I was thirsty, but I waited—dismissing all thoughts of dry futility—because I knew the vendors would soon be among us, offering drinks to reward our parched, but enduring, patience. "Cola-colacola! Co-la! Co-la!" My yearning conjured up the call—it was an auditory hallucination, with no substance or reality. The heat that blasted from our bodies and stuck us to our chairs wrapped us in cocoons of self-absorbed misery. I was at the ballpark with my son, but all I could think about was my growing conviction that, if we didn't drink something soon, we would surely die. With a clarity born of dehydration, I saw our fate: by the time the vendors finally reached us, we would be gone, our thirsting spirits flown. There would be nothing of us left to greet them. The cola woman and the beer man would find nothing but desolation—row after row of desiccated husks, sere and brittle, rattling in the faint breeze that came, like the vendors, too late.

One vendor did eventually drop by, but he was greeted with hoots of derision and looks of sullen reproach and resentment. He—a big, burly, strong-looking fellow—carried no ice-filled tub of liquid refreshment. No, on this blistering day, he was carrying only a fistful of programs. "Pro-o-o-grams! Fourdollarsfora Pro-o-o-gram!" Our eyes pleaded with him; we were too parched to voice our despair aloud. We . . . are . . . thirsty . . . we rasped in silence, willing him to acknowledge our need. Where is the beer guy? Where is the cola lady? The guy with the frozen lemonade? A little Malt Cup Madness would be a big help here, even though we know we'll only be thirstier in the end . . . When the program vendor strolled by a second, then a third time, my patience fled. I'd had enough. I joined the line—no, the mob, the teeming horde, the huddled masses—at the concession stand.

I missed several innings of the ball game while I waited my turn at the stand back in the tunnel. It was hotter there, and we were more crowded than we'd been in our seats. I looked dully at my companions-in-waiting, and wondered how they fared in this hellish exile from the game. Sweat poured down our faces and necks; our handkerchiefs were soon soaked into uselessness. Our shirts clung to our backs like wet leaves on pavement, but the moisture did not cool us. We could see the game on the in-house monitors that hung from the ceiling. One man complained to no one in particular, "I drove six hours to get here. Six hours to stand in a tunnel and watch the game on TV." A six-hour drive meant he was a Cubs fan. It didn't matter; we suffered together, Cubs fans and Tigers fans alike, all funneled together in a stagnant puddle of sweat and thirst and strained endurance. I marveled at the relative coolness of our tempers. Time crept until, at long last, I passed the ordeal. I returned in triumph to the seat beside my son, bearing two enormous paper cups of cola. I had also called upon vestigial memories of Girl Scout preparedness during my time of waiting, and had provided for a future beyond our immediate cola needs. My pockets bulged with bottles of Tiger Water, for which I was offered scalper's prices by scheming fans who hoped, vainly, to avoid confronting their own ordeals. I felt like Gunga Din, the heroic water boy who saved his stranded regiment. Nathan greeted me solemnly on my long-delayed return. "So glad you could join me for the game," he said.

Maybe the heat addled my brain, but I really don't remember many of the details of the game we saw that night. Nathan tells me that I saw Tony Clark hit the ball way out past center field in a three-run homer for the Tigers. He also says we saw a bit of history that night. The Cubs' right fielder that Nathan had been so eager to see turned out to be a happy-looking fellow named Sammy Sosa. I saw him hit a homer straight into the right field upper deck that had everybody on their feet and cheering. I remember this myself because I found that I was yelling and applauding, too. I stopped in confusion and asked Nathan, "Why are we all cheering? Isn't he on the other team?" Yes, he was, and it didn't matter at that particular moment. Sammy Sosa was and is a Chicago Cub; all of us were cheering him because we'd just seen him break the record for the most home runs in a single month. That was in June. Sosa, of course, went on to hit a lot more home runs that summer. I went on to see a few more ball games at Tiger Stadium with Nathan. I know most of the Tigers' line-up now, and I know what their uniforms look like. I rarely get confused and cheer the wrong team anymore.

The vendors came back, too. The crowds that had swept over Tiger Stadium receded after the Cubs left town, and the vendors who were lost reappeared. They'd never really left; it seems they'd just got swallowed up in the inrushing tide of Cubs fans. They still have my affection, those vendors, if not my unquestioning faith. I've become a smuggler now, of sorts, concealing bottled water of my own in the depths of my handbag each time I visit the ballpark.

Nathan is back at college now. We took in one last game together shortly before he left. It was a double-header, but I don't remember who was playing. I do remember that we pulled on jackets against the cool night air part way through the second game, and that the vendors were as attentive to us as waiters in the finest restaurant. And I remember looking back and thinking of all the places that Nathan and I had found to sit in Tiger Stadium over the course of the summer. We'd had seats in right and left field, in the upper and lower decks, even once in the coveted seats of the Tigers Den right behind the Tigers' on-deck circle. They were fine seats, all of them, even the ones that were forsaken by the vendors back when Sammy Sosa came to town. I learned from that experience that the vendors might not always be there. But my memories of that and other ball games seen with Nathan are another matter. Those memories are, to me, more precious than a sip of water, and I have faith that they will stay with me forever.

Apo

Michelle Rebant

He had eyes the color of robin's eggs. Every day my grandpa would feed the birds in his backyard, and if they didn't come right away he'd wait until they did. He had the same routine almost every day until he was sick. He filled an old plastic measuring cup with birdseed in the garage, and then circled around the house to the backyard patio, which was just a slab of cement. It took him awhile to stoop down. But he did eventually and poured the seed in a straight line down the cement. He nodded to himself and went inside through the patio door to wait. Soon the birds would come and start pecking at the food. The bluejays and cardinals would come for the sunflower seeds, but the robins were his favorite. Every spring *he* would see the first robin of the year.

But one year he didn't get to see the robins. When he was seventy-nine years old cancer consumed him in a week. On Monday he was sitting in "his" scratchy tweed chair in front of the TV, kicking it every time static fuzzed up the screen. The next day my grandma drove him to the hospital because he felt like someone was stabbing him in the back. On Sunday he was dead. At the hospital he was so drugged up that he hallucinated mounds of frizzy hair on my head. The last thing he said to me was that I needed a haircut. The last thing he said to my sister was "I'm feeling better already, kiddo." Then she went and cried by the window.

My sister and I called him Apo, which means grandpa in Polish, though I don't think he ever realized what it meant. One time when I walked into the living room, I said "Hi Apo!" and he responded, "Yeah, I'll have a couple of 'em." He thought we were calling him Apple. His hearing was not as sharp as his wit, though. Sometimes he just *pretended* it wasn't as sharp. Once my grandma asked him if he wanted a sandwich. He said yes. "Well, what kind of sandwich?" "A sandwich." "Yes, I know, but what KIND of sandwich?" "A sandwich." By this time she walked off, muttering, "I'll make you ham." To which he promptly yelled, "I want bologna!"

He was prompt and respectable; a thoroughbred. Even when he went to the gas station he still wore his gray felt hat and dress pants. He felt he had to be proper since all of the men in his life were not. His mother was 15 when she had an arranged marriage to his then 39 year-old father. His father was an alcoholic who beat his wife and son, and he eventually walked out on them. My grandpa was put in an orphanage until his mother could take care of him again. While he was there he became ill with scarlet fever and almost died at age nine. That was a wake-up call for my great-grandmother. She took him out of the orphanage and they went to live with her brother and his wife. While living with them Apo's hatred of priests began when one made a pass at his mother during a church bazaar.

He never finished high school because his mother needed him to work to help pay the bills. At seventeen he got a job at an automotive factory and built car parts and machines for Chrysler. He worked there well into his sixties. Every day when he came home from work, my mom told me that he would throw down his lunch tin on the kitchen table and say, "Another day shot to hell."

These aren't your typical grandpa stories. He never told us about his shiny new bike for his paper route, or the time he stole some jam out of the pantry and was caught, or how his mother won the blue ribbon for her apple pie at the county fair, or how his dad campaigned for Woodrow Wilson, because none of that ever happened. He never took me on his knee and gave me a Werther's original and told me how he tasted that sweet, buttery candy for the first time and knew that he was special. Then again, he wasn't Grandpa. He was Apo.

It wasn't just the name, however, that made him different from the typical doting grandfather. When I was very young I didn't understand why Apo wasn't in World War II because every other kid's grandpa was. He was too old for that, my mother said. As I grew older I figured out why he never had any war stories or medals or combat wounds. His battles were fought on the assembly line and his scars went deeper than the skin. He never dropped bombs from a B-52, but that didn't mean he didn't love to fly. The birds he fed flew for him, and he never even had to leave the backyard. Their wings were his way of leaving behind the factory, wage battles, soggy sandwiches, and over-friendly priests without deserting his wife and child. He would not shirk the duty of being a dad as his own father had done.

Years later when he came over to our house for Father's Day, our dog Mikie bit his hand. The blood was flowing down his palm, and he asked me to fetch him a bandage. When I returned I put it in his good hand. He looked at me and said, "What's the matter? You're not going to put it on? How can I do it with one hand?" I didn't even like the *sight* of blood. Putting a little plastic strip over a spewing bloody gash repulsed me. I didn't want to be his nursemaid, plugging up his leaks. I turned my head, squinted my eyes, and quickly slapped the bandage on the moment I hit skin. When I fully opened my eyes, the Bandaid was halfway down his arm. He just looked at me and laughed, and put the bandage on himself.

Soon he relied on me for more than just bringing him bandages. He sat next to my sister Julie and me during our Great Uncle Johnny's funeral. It was a miracle in itself that my grandpa actually went to the funeral since it was in a church. Yet Johnny and Apo were fishing buddies, and Apo was willing to do anything for a "pardner" as they called each other. When it was time for our pew to pass by the coffin and say our final farewells, my sister and I noticed that Apo wasn't behind us. He was still sitting in the pew. Julie went back and whispered, "What's wrong? You're not going to let that priest incident stop you from saying goodbye to your friend, are you?" It wasn't that, he said; he just couldn't get out of the seat. So Julie and I each held an arm while he yanked himself up like a hooked fish. He staggered up to see Johnny whose coffin was full of those red veteran's poppies you can buy at parades and fairs. Apo put his hand on Johnny's chest and said, "Goodbye, kiddo."

A few months later it was my family's turn to say goodbye. Somehow I knew exactly when Apo died. I was trying to fall asleep by thinking of anything but my grandpa lying in a hospital bed dying. At 11:30 p.m. I found myself praying, "Please God, please let him go to heaven. Please forgive him." When I woke up the next morning, my mom was at the foot of the bed. She told me that he had died at 11:34. She described how my grandma stroked his forehead long after he had died and kept saying to herself, "It's still warm. It's still warm."

Two days before Apo died a pastor who was making rounds throughout the hospital came into his room. He knelt down by Apo's bedside with Bible in hand, ready to pray and comfort my grandpa before he died. When Apo saw the pastor, he raised his spotted, trembling hand with the IV tubes drooping down to the bedsheets. Glowering at the pastor with pale, watery blue eyes, he said through clenched teeth, "Get away from me." As I sat with my head on my arms a few feet away from his bed, the same Bible verse kept spinning in my head like a requiem: "Abba, Father, forgive him, for he knows not what he does."

◆

Award Winning Essays
Writing Excellence Award Winners: 2000

Crohn's Disease: *What is the best form of treatment?*

Brian Felice

It is late on a Saturday night. Most people are sound asleep, but not me. I still have a couple of things to take care of before I can go to sleep. My main reason for staying up late tonight is so that I can perform my weekly ritual of filling my pill case. Because of the fact that I sometimes take up to four different medications, totaling thirty pills in one day, it is mandatory that I have a pill case. Without it, I may miss a dose of medication, or even worse, miss a whole set of medications. That is why I take the time every Saturday night to fill my pill case, making sure that each medication is in its proper slot. If I miss one dose of a single medication, I will probably get sick and have a miserable day. Crohn's disease affects people to different extents, but in my specific case it is imperative to my well being that I take my medicine at the proper time and do not miss doses. Drug therapy is one of few treatments available for me at the moment. Since there is no cure for Crohn's, an immune system disease affecting my large intestine, medication is the primary therapy which I can utilize to keep my health and quality of life at a reasonable level.

As mentioned previously, Crohn's disease is an auto-immune disease that affects my large intestine. It is classified as an Inflammatory Bowel Disease (IBD), which includes two other similar diseases. Crohn's disease is a disorder which has potential to effect the entire gastrointestinal tract. In my specific case, the disease has stayed solely in my large intestine and has not spread elsewhere. Of all patients with Crohn's disease, roughly twenty-five percent of these patients will have colon only involvement like myself (Lowes 602). There is always a possibility that the disease may spread, but at the current time it appears that it will stay in this area. It affects my large intestine in the aspect that my immune system does not recognize it as part of my body. My immune system treats my large intestine as a foreign object. When this happens, my body's normal response is to activate the immune system so that my body will be able to fight off and take care of this "foreign object." What my body does not realize is that my large intestine is not foreign and it is attacking a healthy organ and as a result, damaging its tissues. This reaction causes the lining of my large intestine to become inflamed and ulcerated. The inflammation will range in severity depending on the area affected.

Because of the inflammation of the intestinal tissues, several symptoms and problems may occur. The most common symptoms are severe abdominal cramping and diarrhea. Other common symptoms include: malnutrition, weight loss, fever, rectal bleeding, anemia, fatigue, and loss of appetite. Because of the symptoms and the severity of this disease, scientists and researchers are desperately searching for a cure, but at this time their search is coming up empty-handed. Along with not having a cure for Crohn's, researchers do not know what causes this disease either.

The theory that is most commonly accepted is that Crohn's disease is the result of the body's immune system reacting to a virus or bacteria that causes inflammation in the intestine. It is a common misconception that stress or emotional problems cause Crohn's disease. It has been proven that stress does not cause Crohn's disease, rather that the disease itself may cause stress and emotional trauma. Along with being an immune disease, there is some evidence to show that the this disease is also genetic. Of all Crohn's patients, and estimated twenty percent of them will have an immediate family member with some form of Inflammatory Bowel Disease (*Inflammatory*). This raises the idea that Crohn's disease, while most likely being caused by a bacteria, may have hereditary links.

Since scientists have yet to find a cure for Crohn's disease, they are continuously developing new treatments and medications to help patients suppress the disease and manage the symptoms. Since each case of Crohn's disease is different, not all the new medications created are applicable to my specific case. It is my doctor's job to find out what combination of medications and therapies will best suit me and improve my specific condition. G.M. Eisen, a well-respected gastroenterologist, remarks that "The major therapeutic goal for most patients with chronic illness is not a cure of the disease, but rather an improvement in function and quality of life resulting from an alleviation of the illness or from a limitation of the progression of the disease" (quoted in Bodger 19). With technology and science rapidly expanding it is possible that someday in the near future a cure for Crohn's disease will be reached. Until that time, doctors can only treat my disease and hope that my symptoms will go away and that I may enter a period of remission. With all of the different possibilities for treatments available, ranging anywhere from medication to surgery, how does my doctor know which treatment to use and which one will work the best for my specific case?

The medication *Asacol*® was the first medication that my doctor started using to treat me. This medication is classified as a 5-aminosalicylic acid, commonly known as a 5-ASA drug treatment. When first diagnosed with Crohn's disease, this type of therapy and medication was the most logical place to begin. It is the most basic therapy for treating and maintaining mild cases of Crohn's disease. The 5-ASA grouping of medications are all anti-inflammatory treatments. These medications are similar to aspirin except for the fact that it contains a 5-amino group instead of an acetyl group. *Asacol*®, the medication I began on, is a 5-ASA targeted specifically at the large intestine. It contains a coating on it that will not breakdown until it reaches a pH greater than seven. It will not reach this pH until it enters the large intestine, where it will breakdown releasing its anti-inflammatory chemicals throughout the intestine (Bloom 11). Some patients complain of nausea and fever as a result of this medication, but the majority of the patients, including myself, found these medications very tolerable and see no major side effects from this type of treatment. The 5-ASA group of medications have been found to do a great job in reducing the initial inflammation and maintaining the remission it achieves. For this reason, I am still on *Asacol*® today. It might not be effective as an inflammation reducer in my severe case, but it does help my body maintain remission and helps prevent relapses from occurring. Until the day when a cure is found for Crohn's disease, it is likely that I will be on a daily dose of *Asacol*® or another similar 5-ASA medication.

When first becoming sick and needing medical treatment, *Asacol*® was the way to go. It was not until my doctor realized that my case was much more severe that he knew that *Asacol*® and other 5-ASA treatments would not provide significant relief to my disease. 5-ASA's while being one of the most useful drugs for mild disease does not seem to greatly improve the symptoms and inflammation associated with severe cases of Crohn's disease. This led my doctor to another popular form of treatment, corticosteroids. While maintaining 5-ASA treatment, steroids were added to my daily regime of medication.

Steroid treatment is the next logical progression after the basic 5-ASA medications do not respond. Although they work by the same mechanism that 5-ASA medications do, they are much stronger and will have a more immediate effect on the inflammation. It is important to understand how steroids work and why are they are important to the treatment of Crohn's disease. Steroids are strong anti-inflammatory medications. They work by reducing the inflammation in the tissues of affected areas. Due to the fact that steroids are most commonly administered orally, the large intestine is not the only organ which is affected by the steroids. When steroids are taken, the activity of the adrenal glands becomes suppressed. Adrenal glands, when functioning normally, secrete a hormone that contributes to my body's immune system and metabolism. Taking regular doses of steroids replaces the suppressed adrenal glands. This must be considered when tapering off this medication. Without careful tapering of steroid dosage, severe withdrawal symptoms may occur. My body would probably enter a state of shock and most likely relapse out of remission. Although steroid treatment has the potential to be dangerous, under careful administration and monitoring doctors are able to minimize and reduce the risk tremendously.

The side effects from steroid treatment will depend on the specific patient and the dosage amount. When on doses of twenty milligrams or more daily, I notice more dramatic side effects. These effects include rounding of the face, acne, increased appetite, joint pain, irritability, calcium depletion, weight gain, and insomnia. Because of the severe and possibly dangerous side effects involved with steroid treatment, doctors prefer to only use this treatment when necessary and only for the short term. Unlike most 5-ASA medications, steroids are not meant to be used to maintain a remission. Besides the severe side effects, clinical trials have shown that relapses occur for patients who stay on steroids to maintain remission. For this reason, steroid treatment is usually accompanied by some other form of 5-ASA treatment. By combining these two medications my doctor is able to take care of the inflammation with strong steroid treatment, and then use the 5-ASA medication to keep my body in remission.

When my body failed to respond to aggressive steroid treatment, I thought that I was running out of medical options and that surgery would soon be a reality. It was at this time my doctor started me on

Imuran®. This medication, an immunosuppressant, opened a window to a whole new form of therapy and treatment that I did not know was available.

Immunosuppressants work exactly as their name implies. The theory behind immunosuppressants is based on the fact that people with Crohn's disease have an over-active immune system. By suppressing the immune system, my body is not able to attack my large intestine, therefore keeping me in a state of good health. Immunosuppressants are not used until the later stages of treatment for several reasons. Besides its slow onset, immunosuppressants are not meant to be a single therapy. Instead, they are meant to accompany other forms of therapies allowing those treatments to have a greater chance of working. One of the main problems associated with immunosuppressants is the time they take to work. It takes anywhere from three to six months before the effects of this medication can be noticed (Bodger 18). The side effects of immunosuppressants are relatively minimal. The biggest drawback with immunosuppressants is their affect of shutting down the immune system. My body becomes more susceptible to bacteria and viral infections when my immune system is suppressed. If I am to get the flu or some other common illness, my body does not have the ability to fight off this virus because my immune system is "asleep." This makes the common cold, flu, sore throats, and fevers much more dangerous.

Researchers are constantly developing new treatments and therapies for Crohn's disease. The latest of these treatments is Infliximab. The common name for this medication is *Remicade*®. This treatment is different from all other therapies discussed up to this point with respect to its mechanism of action. Most of the other treatments are therapies that concentrate on controlling and treating inflammation associated with Crohn's, whereas *Remicade*® prevents inflammation from beginning.

To understand how *Remicade*® works it is important to understand *tumor necrosis factor alpha (TNF-a)*. This is a pro-inflammatory protein created by the body's immune cells. It is the protein which is thought to cause or contribute to the chronic inflammation associated with Crohn's disease. *Remicade*® is an anti-tumor necrosis factor substance. A medical newsletter states "It is a monoclonal antibody that inhibits tumor necrosis factor" (*Infliximab* 19). By doing this the TNF is removed from the bloodstream before it can reach the large intestine. This helps prevent the possibility of inflammation.

Remicade® is the first medication that has been created solely for the treatment of Crohn's disease. Along with being a treatment specifically for Crohn's, the U.S. Food and Drug Administration restricts the use of this medication "for the treatment of moderate to severe Crohn's disease that does not respond to standard therapies and for the treatment of open, draining fistulas" (*Crohn's Disease* 3). Luckily this treatment is available to me because of the fact that my disease is severe and I have not responded to any other mode of treatment up to this point. I received my first infusion of *Remicade®* in the middle of October this year and will be finding out in a few weeks if it was effective and if I will receive another infusion.

Clinical studies have shown great results accompanied by minimal side effects with this new treatment. The treatment is administered over a two hour period by an intravenous infusion. It is during this time when the majority of the side effects will occur. Fever, chills, increased blood pressure, and headaches are the most common effects associated with the administration of this medication. After the infusion this medication will stay in the body and continue to work for about two months. At that time the treatment is assessed and my doctor will make a determination whether or not to continue this mode of treatment. Studies show that of the patients tested, about fifty percent will enter a remission and over eighty percent will show signs of improvement and relief (*Infliximab* 19) Because of *Remicade's* recent approval, the long term use of this medication is still being studied and evaluated.

When all else fails, surgery becomes inevitable. Surgery is always considered to be the last form of treatment. Surgery is the treatment which is closest to a cure for Crohn's disease. Once the intestine or part of the intestine has been removed it cannot be replaced, which eliminates the option for future advancements and treatments. Surgery is determined on a case by case basis. In the winter of 1998 it was determined by my doctor, my surgeon, my family, and I that surgery was the next and hopefully final step in my battle with Crohn's disease. I had become steroid dependent to the point that I could not be weaned off of them and that my body was addicted to them. This became a deciding factor in determining whether or not to have surgery, due to fact of the severe side effects that accompany steroids. According to my gastroenterologist, Dr. Samir Al-Hadidi, "You were on very high doses of *Prednisone, Imuran®, Asacol®,* and anti-diarrheals and still doing poorly—bleeding, abdominal pain, and diarrhea." By having surgery, chances were that my medications would be drastically decrease, while at the same time increasing my quality of life. It was at this point that I knew surgery was right for me. The only thing left to decide was what type of surgery was appropriate for me.

There are two main types of surgeries available for patients that have Crohn's disease similar to my case. The first is called a *resection* or *subtotal colectomy*. In this surgery the doctor does not remove the entire large intestine. Rather, he removes the areas that have had extreme inflammation or have been susceptible to inflammation. After removing these sections, my surgeon reconnects the intestine. In essence the only thing the doctor is doing is shortening the large intestine by removal of the bad portions. Because the large intestine's main purpose is the removal of water from waste, my body will not be able to remove all the water that it normally should be able to after this surgery. This will create an increased number of bowel movements, but it should still be less than the amount experienced while suffering from the disease. The downside to this surgery is its recurrence rate. Fifty to seventy percent of the patients who have this surgery will usually need more surgery within five to ten years (Becker 387). In the majority of cases this surgery is basically to delay the inevitable of the second type of surgery, the *total colectomy*.

The total colectomy is the surgery that provides the most relief from inflammation and other symptoms related to Crohn's disease. Since the inflammation has stayed in my large intestine for three years my doctor has made the assumption that it is unlikely to spread elsewhere in my gastrointestinal tract. This means that by removing the entire large intestine there will be nothing left to become inflamed and diseased. It is not a cure because there is always the possibility of the disease spreading, but it is the closest treatment to a cure possible. When undergoing a total colectomy, the surgeon will remove the entire large intestine. Once the large intestine is removed, the small intestine is then guided out of my body through a hole created in the lower part of my abdomen. The small intestine is then connected to a bag that will collect waste products. The fact that the normal function of the bowel is lost is the major downside to this type of surgery. However, most patients adapt very well to this surgery and find that they prefer this over the type of life they were leading while being sick.

I have already had a subtotal colectomy. With this surgery I found immediate relief from the symptoms which accompany Crohn's. The surgeon told me that I would probably have five to ten years of relief before needing additional surgery. To the shock of my doctors and I, my case has relapsed just six or seven months following the subtotal colectomy. Because of this uncommon happening, I have become a candidate for a total colectomy that I will probably have during the summer of 2000. Even with the questionable results, I do not regret having the subtotal colectomy. It was worth trying before the doctors decided it was necessary to remove my entire large intestine. It did provide temporary relief and I am grateful for that. It appears that the total colectomy is in my future and I do not have any fears or worries about this surgery. It may be difficult adjusting to the new lifestyle, but I think my quality of life will be increased and my troubles with Crohn's disease will be greatly minimized from that point forward.

As the number of alternative and herbal treatments begin to dominate traditional medical treatment, one can only wonder if there are alternative treatments that work for Crohn's disease. Many people have special pills and concoctions which they claim to be the miracle cure for Crohn's disease. The most proven alternative therapy known at this time is called "fish oil therapy." There has been some evidence found showing that fish oil contains anti-inflammatory properties. This treatment while showing some benefit in preventing relapse has not become overly popular. This is because of the foul odor and the indigestion that can accompany fish. While showing only minor side effects, fish oil therapy did show one severe side effect, an increased susceptibility to bleeding. For these reasons, scientists are currently working on developing this treatment into a form that will attract and benefit more patients.

Another form of treatment that is an alternative to traditional medications and therapies is called "nutritional therapy". The difference between this therapy and other alternative treatments is the fact that nutritional therapy is not meant to take the place of traditional treatment. Rather, it is only meant to supplement the primary form of treatment prescribed by the doctor. Nutritional therapy is different for each individual case. Depending on the severity and location of the flare-up, it may be necessary to take more of one nutritional supplement and less of another. To determine what type of nutritional deficiencies that I have at the time of a flare-up I must first go to my doctor so that he can run some blood tests. The results from these tests help determine what type of nutrition that my body is lacking. From these lab results my doctor will be able to recommend the best additional supplements for my specific case. Nutritional therapy not only provides the body with the nutrients it is lacking, it allows my body to recover more quickly than it normally would be able to recover. Although nutritional therapy may not be a cure or a replacement to additional treatment, it will most likely increase the chances of entering and maintaining a remission.

As I finish filling the last day of medication for the week I cannot help but to look back and think about each of the different medications and treatments that I am currently taking or have taken in my three year battle with Crohn's disease. Did one of these treatments rise above my doctors and my expectations? Were any of the treatments considered complete failures? Most importantly, what treatment or combination of treatments worked best for me? For three years now, my doctor and I have tried several different medications and treatments to get my disease into remission. Through his expertise, he has been able to devise a treatment plan that will best suit my individual case of Crohn's disease. This plan will not only help me at the present time, but it will set the parameters for my treatment in years to come.

Over the past few years I think I have tried the majority of the treatments possible for Crohn's disease. I cannot say that there is one medication, treatment, or therapy that by itself is a miracle cure for Crohn's disease. Rather, I think that it is a delicate balance of medication and careful care which will lead to the most symptom and problem free lifestyle. I have found that the 5-ASA medications are great for keeping my disease in remission, but they do not contribute much to reducing the inflammation because of the severity of my case. By combining 5-ASA medication with steroids my body is able to reduce inflammation and then maintain that state of good health. Due to my dependence on steroids that was developed in my case, it was necessary for immunosuppressants to be added my treatment plan. This allowed my body to be weaned off the steroids while still showing the benefits from these treatments. Once these medications became ineffective, *Remicade®* became an option that will work in some cases. Hopefully, this will prevent inflammation and allow my body to enter a remission. If all medication options do not work or do not live up to the expectations that go along with them, then surgery may be the next best option. While causing a significant lifestyle change, surgery has the potential of tremendously increasing the quality of life by decreasing symptoms and problems dramatically. By balancing all of these therapies, it is possible to live a productive and normal life with only a few problems. Dr. P. Andersson, member of the Division of Surgery and Gastroenterology in Sweden, remarks that "The study showed when medicine and surgery are used on a complementary basis, they can effectively control they symptoms" (Andersson 427). At the present time a careful balance of 5-ASA medication, steroids,

Remicade®, and nutritional supplements is the program which provides the most relief and benefits for my case of Crohn's disease. This program will keep my quality of life at the highest level possible until the time that I am able to have a total colectomy.

Works Consulted

Deventer, SJH et al. "A Short-term study of chimeric monoclonal antibody cAZ to Tumor Necrosis Factor Alpha for Crohn's Disease." *New England Journal of Medicine* 337 (1997): 1029–1035.

Hanauer, SB. "Updating the Approach to Crohn's Disease." *Hospital Practice (Office Edition) 34* (15 August 1999): 77–78, 81–83, 87–93.

Inflammatory Bowel Disease. Videocassette. Stanley Riepe. Network for Continuing Medical Education, 1998. 60 min.

Lichtiger, S et al. "Cyclosporine in Severe Ulcerative Colitis Refractory to Steroid Therapy." *New England Journal of Medicine* 330 (1994): 1841–1845.

Lochs, H et al. "Anti-TNF Antibody in Crohn's Disease—Status of Information, Comments and Recommendations on an International Working Group." *Z Gastroenterol (XU1)* 37.6 (1999): 509–512.

Moses, PL et al. "Inflammatory Bowel Disease; Part 2: Current and Future Therapeutic Options." *Postgraduate Medicine 103* (21 May 1998): 86–88, 90, 95, 97, 101.

Mouser, JF and JS Hyams. "Infliximab: A Novel Chimeric Monoclonal Antibody for the Treatment of Crohn's Disease." *Clin Ther (CPE)* 21.6 (1999): 932–942.

Present, DH et al. "Treatment of Crohn's Disease with 6-mercaptopurine: A Long-term, Randomized, Double-blind study." *New England Journal of Medicine* 302 (1980): 981–987.

Works Cited

Al-Hadidi, Samir. Personal interview. 10 Nov. 1999.

Andersson, P et al. "Low Symptomatic Load in Crohn's Disease with Surgery and Medicine as Complementary Treatments." *Scandinavian Journal of Gastroenterology* 33.4 (1998): 423–430.

Becker, JM. "Surgical Therapy for Ulcerative Colitis and Crohn's Disease." *Gastroenterol Clinic North America (GNA)* 28.2 (1999): 371–390.

Bloom, Michael et al. *Inflammatory Bowel Disease FAQ v3.1* 12 Oct. 1999. 12 Nov. 1999 <http://ibdfaq.freeshell.org>.

Bodger, K et al. "Clinical Economics Review: Medical Management of Inflammatory Bowel Disease." *Alimentary Pharmacology and Therapeutics* 13.1 (1999): 15.

Crohn's Disease. Bethesda, MD: National Digestive Diseases Information Clearinghouse, 1992. 14 Nov. 1999 <http://www.niddk.nih.gov/health/digest/pubs/crohns/crohns.htm>.

Inflammatory Bowel Disease: Diagnosis and Management of Crohn's Disease and Ulcerative Colitis. Videocassette. Daniel H. Present. Network for Continuing Medical Education, 1998. 60 min.

"Infliximab (Remicade) for Crohn's Disease." *Medical Letter on Drugs and Therapeutics* 1.47 (1999): 9–10.

Lowes, F.R. "Crohn's Disease of the Large Intestine." *Inflammatory Bowel Disease* New York, NY: Pearson Professional Limited, 1997: 601–613.

Of Men and Of Ice

Alicia Sanzica

I walked awkwardly across the rubber matted floor to my locker. As I pulled my bag out, Karrie came rushing up to me. I pulled a sweatshirt over my tiny leotard and skirt that hardly covered my butt and took off my gloves.

"Hey, Alicia, my parents are having an ice skating party on our canal tomorrow. Want to come?" she asked me as she slipped skate guards over her blades.

"Ummm. . . . Not really. No offense, but I can't," I said to my friend.

"Why not?" she replied.

"I'm afraid of the ice," I said. She looked at me quizzically as I sat down and began to unlace my well worn three hundred dollar figure skates.

"But, um, you're a figure skater."

"I know, but I'm afraid of ice. I never go on it," I answered.

"Okay, I'm confused. I watch you skate here at the arena three times a week. How can you be afraid of ice?" she asked.

"Whatever. I just am." I grabbed my bag and put on my red, white, and blue jacket that proudly stated "Mt. Clemens Figure Skating" and walked out the door before Karrie could ask any more questions. When I got home, I walked out to my backyard. I sat bundled up on the edge of our sea wall and stared out across the vast white expanse that was Lake St. Clair in the winter time. On an incredibly clear spring day I can see Canada from my bedroom window, but not today, not in the winter. All I could see was white snow drifting across the frozen water and the clear area my dad shoveled off for my hockey playing brother and his friends. I felt foolish. Here I was one of the most prominent skaters at Mt. Clemens Ice Arena and I was too scared to go out on the lake. The mere thought of stepping out onto open ice made my heart drop into my stomach. I never used to be this way, fearing the ice and detesting the cold. In fact when I was younger, I was the first one out in the snow and the last one in. I actually learned to skate on this lake. Now I avoided going outdoors in the wintertime as much as possible and I couldn't be paid enough to venture more than an arm's length from the safety of the sea wall.

I wanted to go to Karrie's party, I really did, but I knew that I would never get off the grass and I'd look like a fool. Eventually I began to lose feeling in my fingers, so I got up and went in the house. My tennis shoes left a trail of hard packed snow behind me, but I didn't care. I sat at the kitchen window and stared at the ice. A plan was forming in my head; I knew what I was going to do. I would go to that party and I would skate. I just had to do something first. As the sun began to set, I got ready. I pulled on my figure skating tights and a pair of thermal underwear. Over this I pulled my skimpy black skating dress and big fleece sweatshirt. I put on my winter hat and a pair of wool mittens. I grabbed my skates and waddled to the door where my boots were. I walked past my parents in the living room without a word. What a sight I must have been to my parents: knit hat, mittens, big fluffy sweatshirt, skating skirt that was incredibly short, and blue flowered thermal underwear. I walked with a determined pace to the sea wall. I had to take off my mittens to tie my skates. I did this very quickly before my hands went numb. I sat in the snow for a few minutes trying to relax myself. Before I could change my mind, I slowly slid off the iron breaker and onto the ice, well actually a snow mound. I grabbed the edge of the wall as my stomach dropped to my knees. I had this horrible weak feeling all over my body. I figured that if I ever made it to the clear patch, that I'd be shaking too much to actually skate. I forced myself to let go and I began my slow walk to the ice, leaving an odd trail of slashes in the snow. I hadn't been this far from the wall since that February afternoon seven years ago. It seemed like an eternity by the time I reached the ice. By this time, I was convinced that my heart would explode; it was beating so fast.

My well sharpened blades slid slowly across the ice. My hands went numb with fear. I used my training to slow myself to a stop. I looked back and saw the sea wall. It was only ten feet away, but to me it looked ten miles. My heart stopped beating for a second. I took a few deep breaths and calmed myself down. I took a few cautious glides forward. The familiar feeling of my blades cutting ice flowed through my body. It was a feeling I lived for and knew so well. As my second nature took over, I began to relax. I did a few slow spins and a couple of lazy laps around the homemade rink. I was convincing myself that everything was okay.

"Hey. I'm on the ice. Cool," I nervously said aloud to myself. "I can go to the party after all . . ." I stopped mid-sentence because at that moment the ice began to crack. It was only the booming sound that ice makes when it freezes further and bends with pressure. It was no where near me, but I began to scream. I collapsed to the ice and hugged the surface. It was as if that day, years ago, was happening all over again.

The bright sun glared off of the whiteness around us. My dad and I trudged across the frozen ice. He was lugging his ice fishing gear and I was carrying my skates. I pulled my sunglasses out of my pocket and put them on my twelve year old face. I loved to go out on the ice with my dad. I could skate all day even though it scared all the fish away. It was okay because my dad never caught anything anyway. We just went to spend time together and so he could make up stories about the big one that got away. It was just another one of those winter days. We trudged more than a mile off shore to one of his favorite spots, the sand dunes. If you were careless with your boat in the summer, you could easily run it aground here. He told me that in some places it was only three feet deep, in others it was as deep as fifteen. He drilled his hole through the ice and I put my skates on. We went about our business for two hours before we both got too cold to stay out there. My dad gathered his equipment and filled the hole with snow. He spray-painted it with a giant orange X to warn other fishermen of the open hole. We headed back to shore. We came back a little further to our left than we were when we had gone out. That's why we never saw the hole before. We were laughing and joking that way kids and their dads do. Suddenly, the ice was gone from under me. I was falling into open water. Everything happened in slow motion, yet so fast at the same time. I screamed as I watched my dad disappear from my sight. My vision clouded as icy cold water swirled above my head. Water soaked through my clothes, weighting me down, pulling me further and further from the opening above me. Weak winter sunlight drifted though the murky green water. I tried to swim for the hole, but my clothes were too heavy. I clawed blindly at the water around me. The ice boomed above me as it buckled under my father's weight. He came crashing through the ice. He swam towards me. I couldn't see him, but I felt him grab the back of my jacket and pull me up. My lungs were burning to exhale. I couldn't hold my breath any longer and I took a deep breath. This was a big mistake to do under water. At this point I realized the vast difference between us and fish. Water filled my mouth and lungs. I choked and gagged, which only made things worse. Suddenly, we broke the surface. I coughed and spit water, gulping greedy breaths of air. I clung to my father as he treaded water in the icy hole. He pulled me to the edge of the ice and shoved, pulled, and pushed me onto the ice. I just laid there flat on my belly and cried. By this time, other fishermen had seen what happened and came to our aid. They set up a human chain, each man laying on his stomach holding onto another's ankles. I felt strong arms pull me away from the break in the ice and towards an awaiting snowmobile. They must have helped my dad out because he was right behind me. I kept crying and crying.

"You're okay now honey. Don't you worry," some kindly fisherman said as he took off his coat and draped it over me. On the ride back to shore, I watched fascinated as the steam began to rise off my body. I was so cold that my body was producing extra heat in an attempt to warm me up. I didn't realize that I was shivering uncontrollably. We eventually made it back and someone drove us home. My mother rushed me into a warm bath and dry clothes. Thankfully we were okay, although we had lost my skates and my dad's equipment. I vowed never to go near open ice again.

And I held true to that vow, until today that is. I laid on the ice sobbing and screaming until my dad came running out. He picked me up and carried me into the house. My mom wrapped a warm blanket around my shoulders and held me until I stopped crying. I knew that I would not be going to Karrie's party tomorrow nor would I ever try to overcome my fear of ice again.

It's All Relative: A Study of Kinship Term Acquisition

Janet Steigerwald

Introduction

It has often been established that word meanings gradually develop with age (Benson and Anglin 41). Children's word meanings do not always match those of the adults around them because the lexical entries for early words in a child's vocabulary are often incomplete. Children add semantic features to lexical entries in a regular and predictable manner. The words that are more complex semantically will be the ones that are learned later by the child acquiring language (Haviland and Clark 23, 24). The data in this study showed very little agreement with data of previous studies that suggest a relationship between the number of relational components in a kinship term and their predicted order of acquisition. However, a relationship was shown between the increase in a child's age and the sophistication of kinship term definitions. If all confounding variables were removed, it is likely that this study would illustrate that the relative complexity of terms belonging to the same semantic field can be used to make predictions about their order of acquisition.

Review of Literature

Kinship terms represent a semantic field with different semantic and conceptual properties than other nouns. While object names are referential terms that denote objects or classes of objects, kinship terms are relational words that describe an individual's position within a family (Benson and Anglin 42). Within the area of kinship term acquisition, there are studies claiming that experience (environment) is the key to the order of acquisition, and other studies that dispute this, claiming semantic complexity is the key.

Nancy Benson and Jeremy Anglin conducted a study that concentrated on how experience affected word learning and concept formation in the area of kinship term acquisition. Benson and Anglin's cross-sectional study of the acquisition of kinship terms included interviews of five groups of subjects (three, four, five, and six year-olds as well as adults). Each group consisted of four males and four females questioned with respect to their knowledge of kinship terms (Benson and Anglin 41). A parental questionnaire was used to establish the estimated time the subjects had spent with each relation, heard the term spoken, and spoken the term themselves. The results of the Benson and Anglin study showed that experience (environment), not semantic complexity, was a better predictor of the order of kinship term acquisition (Benson and Anglin 61).

Jean Piaget conducted cross-sectional studies on the acquisition of kinship terms as early as 1928. The data from Piaget's large scale research suggested that there were different stages in a child's development of definitions of kinship terms or concepts. A Stage One definition was the most basic and consisted of property features. In a Stage One definition, a "brother" would simply be a male. Stage Two definitions were relational in nature. The child in this stage would know that a brother could exist only if a set of parents had more than one child. Reciprocity was added in Stage Three definitions. The child in this stage realizes that in order to be a brother, you must also have a brother or sister (Haviland and Clark 38). When eliciting verbal responses from children as was done in Piaget's study, it is important to keep in mind that verbal responses depend on abstract reasoning which develops later in children than more concrete knowledge (Chambers and Tavuchis 76).

A large scale cross-sectional study by Danziger in 1957 also collected data by recording the verbal responses of children to questions about kinship terms (Haviland and Clark 25). Danziger found four stages in the development of kinship term definition. The Categorical, Concrete Relational, and Abstract Relational stages that he found corresponded very closely to the three stages identified by Piaget. Danziger however, included a Pre-Categorical stage which he found to be an even earlier stage in kinship term acquisition. A child in the Pre-Categorical stage would define "brother" by simply giving the name of his brother (Haviland and Clark 25). Danziger's results suggest differences among kinship terms that result in some being acquired before others. If we are to relate this fact to the semantic acquisition hypothesis, we should find the lexical entries for some kinship terms are more complex than others.

Different levels of semantic complexity can be assigned to kinship terms when they are analyzed through the study of their relational components and how these components function within the lexicon (Haviland and Clark 29). The complexity of a kinship term is partially based on the number of its relational components. Relational components are combined with simple property features to produce lexical entries. The relational components of kinship are what define a term as being a child of, a parent of, or a spouse of someone else. The other part of kinship term classification is dependent on how many of these components must combine to give the correct meaning to the term (Haviland and Clark 36).

The following is a breakdown of terms used in this study according to their relational components:

Level I	Mother	X parent of Y (X = female)
One	Father	X parent of Y (X = male)
relational	Daughter	X child of Y (X = female)
component	Son	X child of Y (X = male)
	Wife	X spouse of Y (X = female)
	Husband	X spouse of Y (X = male)
Level II	Grandmother	X parent of Y; Y parent of A (X = female)
Same component	Grandfather	X parent of Y; Y parent of A (X = male)
recursed		
Level III	Sister	X child of A; A parent of Y (X = female)
Entries with more than one	Brother	X child of A; A parent of Y (X = male)
relational component		
Level IV	Aunt	X child of A; A parent of B; B parent of Y (X = female)
Entries with two	Uncle	X child of A; A parent of B; B parent of Y (X = male)
components plus recursion		

(Haviland and Clark 36)

If the semantic acquisition hypothesis is correct, Level I kinship terms will be acquired first, followed by those in Level II, Level III, and finally Level IV.

Methodology

Three groups of subjects (3–4 year olds, 5–6 year olds, and 7–9 year olds) with one male and one female per group were interviewed individually and questioned with respect to their knowledge of twelve kinship terms: mother, father, daughter, son, wife, husband, grandmother, grandfather, sister, brother, aunt, and uncle. Three questions were asked about each of the kinship terms. The kinship terms were presented in a random order and the three questions were asked in a consistent order, as follows:

1) 'What is a(n) _____?',
2) 'Tell me everything you know about a(n) _____.', and
3) 'What kind of a thing is a(n) _____?'.

Responses were analyzed for relational components and classified into categories. A Category 1 rating was given when the child did not know what the term meant, named a specific person only, or was blatantly wrong or irrelevant. When a child used property features such as sex or age to define a term, it was given a Category 2 rating. A relational definition (one making use of phrases such as "parent of", or "child of") without reciprocity was given a Category 3 rating. Knowledge that a relationship has a complement is called reciprocity. For example, when "aunt" is defined as one of your parent's siblings, a reciprocal definition would be that an aunt is the parent of nieces or nephews. When a child made use of relational components with reciprocity a Category 4 rating was assigned.

The interviews were conducted in the homes of the children. In all cases, the questions were asked of the child by the child's mother. This kept the point of view of the responses consistent from child to child. Since young children are often most at ease interacting with their own parent, this also helped insure a better quality of response. The researcher was present at all interviews and did the actual recording (on paper) of the childrens' responses. In the case of the youngest children, the questions could be asked a few at a time if the child appeared to be losing interest or becoming distracted. (See Appendix A for transcripts of the childrens' responses.)

A short questionnaire was given to the child's parent to fill out as well. For the eight types of relatives in this study that a child could have (mother, father, sister, brother, aunt, uncle, grandmother, and grandfather), the parent was asked to choose one of four statements as being the most accurate. The choices were as follows: 1) my child does not have a relative of this type, 2) my child has such a relative but has never seen him/her, 3) my child has such a relative but seldom sees him/her, or 4) my child has such a relative and sees him/her often. For the relatives that a child could not actually have (daughter, son, wife, husband), the parent was asked whether the child had heard the term spoken and whether the child had ever spoken the term. When analyzing the data from the childrens' responses, the parental questionnaire was used to determine whether certain results or patterns of results were random or caused by environmental factors. (See Appendix B for parental questionnaires.)

Results

The twelve definitions given by each of the six children were sorted into categories according to the criteria outlined in the methodology section. When a definition included features of more than one category, the definition was not counted twice but was ranked in the highest category for which it qualified. A Category 3 (relational) definition would often contain property features, which are elements of a Category 2 definition as well. Table I shows the breakdown of definitions into categories.

Table I

	Child 1 (F) 3;5	Child 2 (M) 3;7	Child 3 (F) 5;6	Child 4 (M) 6;0	Child 5 (M) 7;2	Child 6 (F) 8;8
Mother	1	2	1	2	4	3
Father	1	1	2	2	3	3
Daughter	1	1	2	2	4	3
Son	1	1	1	1	3	3
Wife	1	1	2	2	3	3
Husband	1	1	2	2	3	3
Grandmother	1	3	1	1	3	4
Grandfather	1	1	1	1	3	3
Sister	1	1	2	2	3	2
Brother	1	1	2	2	3	3
Aunt	1	2	2	1	3	4
Uncle	1	2	1	1	3	3

Category 1: Child does not know what a term means, names a specific person, or is blatantly wrong or irrelevant.

Category 2: Child uses property features such as sex or age to define terms.

Category 3: Child uses relational definitions without reciprocity.

Category 4: Child uses relational and reciprocal definitions.

Table II shows the frequency of the different categories of definition by age group. There is a shift, with age, away from Category 1 definitions (which dominate in the 3–4 age group) towards Category 3 definitions (which dominate the 7–9 age group).

Table II

| Age | Group | N | Category of Definition | | | |
			Category 1	Category 2	Category 3	Category 4
(3–4)	I	2	20	3	1	—
(5–6)	II	2	10	14	—	—
(7–9)	III	2	—	1	19	4
	Totals →→		30	18	20	4

As age increases, there is a decrease in Category 1 definitions and an increase among those in Categories 2 and 3. The rare instances of Category 4 definitions were recorded only for those children in the highest age group.

Tabulations were also carried out to show the frequency of categories of definition for each individual kinship term by age group.

Mother

| Age Group | Category of Definition | | | |
	1	2	3	4
I (3–4)	1	1	—	—
II (5–6)	1	1	—	—
III (7–9)	—	—	1	1
Σ	2	2	1	1

Father

| Age Group | Category of Definition | | | |
	1	2	3	4
I (3–4)	2	—	—	—
II (5–6)	—	2	—	—
III (7–9)	—	—	2	—
Σ	2	2	2	—

Daughter

Age Group	Category of Definition			
	1	*2*	*3*	*4*
I (3–4)	2	—	—	—
II (5–6)	—	2	—	—
III (7–9)	—	—	1	1
Σ	2	2	1	1

Son

Age Group	Category of Definition			
	1	*2*	*3*	*4*
I (3–4)	2	—	—	—
II (5–6)	2	—	—	—
III (7–9)	—	—	2	—
Σ	4	—	2	—

Wife

Age Group	Category of Definition			
	1	*2*	*3*	*4*
I (3–4)	2	—	—	—
II (5–6)	—	2	—	—
III (7–9)	—	—	2	—
Σ	2	2	2	—

Husband

Age Group	Category of Definition			
	1	*2*	*3*	*4*
I (3–4)	2	—	—	—
II (5–6)	—	2	—	—
III (7–9)	—	—	2	—
Σ	2	2	2	—

Grandmother

Age Group	Category of Definition			
	1	*2*	*3*	*4*
I (3–4)	1	—	1	—
II (5–6)	2	—	—	—
III (7–9)	—	—	1	1
S	3	—	2	1

Grandfather

Age Group	Category of Definition			
	1	*2*	*3*	*4*
I (3–4)	2	—	—	—
II (5–6)	2	—	—	—
III (7–9)	—	—	2	—
Σ	4	—	2	—

Sister

Age Group	Category of Definition			
	1	*2*	*3*	*4*
I (3–4)	2	—	—	—
II (5–6)	—	2	—	—
III (7–9)	—	1	1	—
Σ	2	3	1	—

Brother

Age Group	Category of Definition			
	1	*2*	*3*	*4*
I (3–4)	2	—	—	—
II (5–6)	—	2	—	—
III (7–9)	—	—	2	—
Σ	2	2	2	—

Aunt

Age Group	Category of Definition			
	1	2	3	4
I (3–4)	1	1	—	—
II (5–6)	1	1	—	—
III (7–9)	—	—	1	1
Σ	2	2	1	1

Uncle

Age Group	Category of Definition			
	1	2	3	4
I (3–4)	1	1	—	—
II (5–6)	2	—	—	—
III (7–9)	—	—	2	—
Σ	3	1	2	—

From these tables, the mean level of definition for each term can be determined.

Table III shows that as the child's age increases, the mean level of definition also increases. The hypothesis stating that less complex kinship terms should precede more complex ones in order of acquisition is not substantiated by this data set.

Table III

Kin Term	Age Group			
	I (3–4)	II (5–6)	III (7–9)	Mean
Mother	1.5	1.5	3.5	2.16
Father	1	2	3	2.0
Daughter	1	2	3.5	2.16
Son	1	1	3	1.66
Wife	1	2	3	2.0
Husband	1	2	3	2.0
Grandmother	2	1	3.5	2.16
Grandfather	1	1	3	1.66

Table III *(Continued)*

Kin Term	I (3–4)	II (5–6)	III (7–9)	Mean
		Age Group		
Sister	1	2	2.5	1.83
Brother	1	2	3	2.0
Aunt	1.5	1.5	3.5	2.16
Uncle	1.5	1	3	1.83
	1.21	1.58	3.12	

Finally, tabulations were carried out to compare the definitions of the male subjects to those of the female subjects. Frequency of definition categories were figured for each of the twelve kinship terms.

Mother

Sex	1	2	3	4
	Category of Definition			
Male	—	2	—	1
Female	2	—	1	—
Σ	2	2	1	1

Father

Sex	1	2	3	4
	Category of Definition			
Male	1	1	1	—
Female	1	1	1	—
Σ	2	2	2	—

Daughter

Sex	Category of Definition			
	1	*2*	*3*	*4*
Male	1	1	—	1
Female	1	1	1	—
Σ	2	2	1	1

Son

Sex	Category of Definition			
	1	*2*	*3*	*4*
Male	2	—	1	—
Female	2	—	1	—
Σ	3	—	3	—

Wife

Sex	Category of Definition			
	1	*2*	*3*	*4*
Male	1	1	1	—
Female	1	1	1	—
Σ	2	2	2	—

Husband

Sex	Category of Definition			
	1	*2*	*3*	*4*
Male	1	1	1	—
Female	1	1	1	—
Σ	2	2	2	—

Grandmother

Sex	Category of Definition			
	1	*2*	*3*	*4*
Male	1	—	2	—
Female	2	—	—	1
Σ	3	—	2	1

Grandfather

Sex	Category of Definition			
	1	*2*	*3*	*4*
Male	2	—	1	—
Female	2	—	1	—
Σ	4	—	2	—

Sister

Sex	Category of Definition			
	1	*2*	*3*	*4*
Male	1	1	1	—
Female	1	2	—	—
Σ	2	3	1	—

Brother

Sex	Category of Definition			
	1	*2*	*3*	*4*
Male	1	1	1	—
Female	1	1	1	—
Σ	2	2	2	—

Aunt

Sex	Category of Definition			
	1	*2*	*3*	*4*
Male	1	1	1	—
Female	1	1	—	1
Σ	2	2	1	1

Uncle

Sex	Category of Definition			
	1	*2*	*3*	*4*
Male	1	1	1	—
Female	2	—	1	—
Σ	3	1	2	—

Table IV

Kin Term	Gender	
	Male	*Female*
Mother	2.66	1.66
Father	2.0	2.0
Daughter	2.33	2.0
Son	1.66	1.66
Wife	2.0	2.0
Husband	2.0	2.0
Grandmother	2.33	2.0
Grandfather	1.66	1.66
Sister	2.0	1.66
Brother	2.0	2.0
Aunt	2.0	2.33
Uncle	2.0	1.66
	2.053	1.885

The mean level of definition for each term according to subject gender is shown in Table IV. The definitions given by the male subjects were equal to or surpassed the complexity of the definitions given by female subjects for eleven out of twelve kinship terms.

Discussion

When utilizing relational components to determine the semantic complexity of kinship terms, their order of acquisition can be predicted if the semantic complexity hypothesis is indeed valid. The six kinship terms in this study with only one relational component each (mother, father, daughter, son, wife, husband) should be acquired first. The next group of terms acquired should be those with the same component recursed (grandmother, grandfather), followed by terms with more than one relational component (sister, brother). Finally, the kinship terms with two relational components plus recursion will be learned (aunt, uncle).

When categorizing the child's definitions, as was done in this study, the arrival at a more complex or sophisticated definition signaled the child's acquisition of a kinship term. The data collected in this study showed that as the age of the child increased, the clarity and sophistication of the definitions improved. This supports the theory that as children get older, they add semantic features to words in their lexicon in a predictable manner. However, the children in this study acquired the twelve kinship terms in a more or less random order, lending no support to the use of relational components as a measure of semantic complexity. Rather than taking this conclusion at face value, confounding variables must be discussed.

The responses of the children in this study were transcribed, analyzed, and categorized by one researcher. The majority of the previous studies on this subject are collaborative efforts of at least two researchers. When working alone, it is possible that the researcher loses important input and feedback on things such as categorization choices, statistical computations, and data interpretation.

The participants in this study, chosen largely with respect to their familiarity and convenience to the researcher, had surprisingly similar backgrounds. They all came from traditional nuclear families of middle to upper-middle class incomes. All children surveyed also had mothers who did not work outside the home. One of the variables among the children, which was at no point figured into the results, was individual IQ differences. In a study of this size, the importance of using children of equal (or similar) IQ cannot be overlooked. If this study were to be replicated with thirty children from each of the three age groups, matching the IQ of each child becomes less of an issue because of the mathematical law of averages.

An unexpected finding of this study was that the male subjects defined eleven out of the twelve kinship terms with equal or greater accuracy than the female subjects. The only term that the females had superior definitions for was "aunt". Environmental factors cannot be used to explain this because, according to the parental surveys, the male children all had aunts that they saw frequently, while one of the females did not even see her aunts on a regular basis. The parental surveys showed that all of the children in this study had most of the types of kin and saw them often. Four of the six children did not have a sister, yet one of those four children gave the most sophisticated definition for "sister". One of the two children without a brother gave the most accurate definition for "brother". The five year old child who seldom saw her aunt, gave a better definition for that term than a six year old who saw his aunts on a regular basis. These findings support the conclusion that the environment is not a factor in kinship term acquisition.

Overall, the highest mean level of definition went to female kinship terms (mother, daughter, grandmother, aunt, wife). The only female kinship term that did not make this list was "sister". The fact that four of the six children in this study did not have a sister could be proposed as an environmentally related explanation for this. It can just as quickly be refuted by the fact that the highest level of definition for "sister" went to a child without a sister. An alternate explanation might be that since it was the mothers in this study who elicited the definitions, the children were somehow more tuned in to a female perspective. Perhaps being questioned by a female helped the subjects to more accurately recall information about other females.

Conclusion

The data in this study was collected through interviews composed of questions about the definitions of twelve kinship terms and conducted with children. Because verbal responses depend upon abstract reasoning, simply asking a child for definitions may be a good method of gathering preliminary data, but not the best method of assessing how much that child actually knows about the meaning of each kinship term.

The idea that children enrich and solidify their knowledge of known words by establishing links among words and concepts is not a new one (Pan and Gleason 142). Assigning meaning to new words involves a process of comparing old to new semantic knowledge and augmenting a pre-existing semantic system with this knowledge (Pan and Gleason 129). In the area of kinship term acquisition, studies have consistently revealed a qualitative change in the definitions and descriptions produced by children of increasing age levels (Benson and Anglin 44). The data from this study clearly shows support of this.

Contrary to the findings of Benson and Anglin, the results of this study showed no link between experience (environment) and kinship term acquisition. It would seem plausible then, to hypothesize that the results would show that the semantic complexity theory explains kinship term acquisition. However, assigning an order of acquisition to kinship terms based on the use of relational components as a measure of semantic complexity was not supported by the data of this study. Due to the many confounding variables at work, this lack of support for the semantic complexity theory should be regarded cautiously.

Works Cited

Benson, Nancy J., and Jeremy Anglin. "The Child's Knowledge of English Kin Terms." *First Language* 7 (1987): 41–66.

Chambers, James C., and Nicholas Tavuchis. "Kids and Kin: Children's Understanding of American Kin Terms." *Journal of Child Language* 3 (1976): 63–80.

Haviland, Susan E., and Eve Clark. "'This Man's Father is My Father's Son': A Study of the Acquisition of English Kin Terms." *Journal of Child Language* 1 (1974): 23–47.

Pan, Barbara Alexander, and Jean Berko Gleason. "Semantic Development: Learning the Meanings of Words." *Development of Language* (4th ed.). Ed. Jean Berko Gleason. Needham Heights, MA: Allyn & Bacon, 1997: 122–158.

Appendix A—Children's Responses

Subject #1 (female)—Age: 3 years, 5 months

What is a mother?	I don't want to.
Tell me all you know about mothers.	No.
What type of a thing is a mother?	I don't know.
What is a husband?	
Tell me all you know about husbands.	
What type of a thing is a husband?	
What is an aunt?	Our friend.
Tell me all you know about aunts.	Our friends.
What type of a thing is an aunt?	
What is a sister?	My brothers.
Tell me all you know about sisters.	
What type of a thing is a sister?	
What is a father?	Friend.
Tell me all you know about fathers.	
What type of a thing is a father?	
What is a son?	Friend.

Subject #1 (continued)

Tell me all you know about sons.	Friends.
What type of a thing is a son?	
What is a grandmother?	No.
Tell me all you know about grandmothers.	
What type of a thing is a grandmother?	
What is an uncle?	I don't know. I'm eating my apple.
Tell me all you know about uncles.	
What type of a thing is an uncle?	Don't know.
What is a wife?	
Tell me all you know about wives.	I don't know.
What type of a thing is a wife?	
What is a brother?	A sister.
Tell me all you know about brothers.	
What type of a thing is a brother?	I can't tell you because I'm drinking my milk.
What is a daughter?	I don't know.
Tell me all you know about daughters.	Uh uh.
What type of a thing is a daughter?	I don't know.

What is a grandfather?	I don't know.
Tell me all you know about grandfathers.	Uh uh.
What type of a thing is a grandfather?	A sons.

Subject #2 (male)—Age: 3 years, 7 months

What is a mother?	Big, girl, Omi
Tell me all your know about mothers.	They play with you. They work.
What type of a thing is a mother?	Daddy.
What is a husband?	
Tell me all you know about husbands.	Your family—when you both live together and live inside the same house.
What type of a thing is a husband?	
What is an aunt?	Girl, Aunt Kim, Aunt Heather
Tell me all you know about aunts.	Work.
What type of a thing is an aunt.	
What is a sister?	A brother.
Tell me all you know about sisters.	
What type of a thing is a sister?	I don't know.

Subject #2 (continued)

What is a father?	Goes with a mother and he works.
Tell me all you know about fathers.	Daddy, Uncle Barth. They work and clean the kitchen.
What type of a thing is a father?	
What is a son?	
Tell me all you know about sons.	
What type of a thing is a son?	
What is a grandmother?	She is a mother. You call her mom.
Tell me all you know about grandmothers.	Omi is daddy's mommy. They are nice. They work.
What type of a thing is a grandmother?	She is a girl. She loves me.
What is an uncle?	Uncle Barth, Uncle Dave, Uncle Norman.
Tell me all you know about uncles.	They work. They slide on the slide.
What type of a thing is an uncle?	He is a boy.
What is a wife?	Mommy.
Tell me all you know about wives.	
What type of a thing is a wife?	
What is a brother?	
Tell me all you know about brothers.	

Subject #2 (continued)

What type of a thing is a brother?	
What is a daughter?	
Tell me all you know about daughters.	
What type of a thing is a daughter?	
What is a grandfather?	Grandpa Jack.
Tell me all you know about grandfathers.	He pumps the fire in the fireplace.
What type of a thing is a grandfather?	

Subject #3 (female)—Age: 5 years, 6 months

What is a mother?	I don't know. Somebody who takes care of children.
Tell me all you know about mothers.	They have to take care of the kids.
What type of a thing is a mother?	
What is a husband?	It's a dad that takes care of kids.
Tell me all you know about husbands.	Anything? They have to work a lot. They have to write a lot of bills.
What type of a thing is a husband?	A boy.
What is an aunt?	I don't know.

Subject #3 (continued)

Tell me all you know about aunts.	Aunt Colleen. Aunt Mary.
What type of a thing is an aunt?	A girl.
What is a sister?	It's a sister.
Tell me all you know about sisters.	Sisters are nice. Sisters share stuff.
What type of a thing is a sister?	It's a girl.
What is a father?	It's a boy.
Tell me all you know about fathers.	They have to work a lot. They have to write a lot of bills.
What type of a thing is a father?	It's a person.
What is a son?	It's a brother. A son is a brother.
Tell me all you know about sons.	They're brothers.
What type of a thing is a son?	Oh boy.
What is a grandmother?	I forgot. I don't know.
Tell me all you know about grandmothers.	I know nothing.
What type of a thing is a grandmother?	I have no clue.
What is an uncle?	A grandpa.
Tell me all you know about uncles.	They drink water. They watch TV.
What type of a thing is an uncle?	A person.

Subject #3 (continued)

What is a wife?	A mom.
Tell me all you know about wives.	I don't know. They have to work a lot. Vacuum, clean, wipe the table off, wash the dishes, wash the clothes.
What type of a thing is a wife?	A woman.
What is a brother?	A son is the same thing as a brother, but I think sons are smaller than brothers.
Tell me all you know about brothers.	I don't know.
What type of a thing is a brother?	A boy.
What is a daughter?	A daughter is a girl.
Tell me all you know about daughter.	I think we already did this. Are daughters the same as sisters? They share nice.
What type of a thing is a daughter?	A girl.
What is a grandfather?	A grandpa.
Tell me all you know about grandfathers.	They watch TV a lot. That's all.
What type of a thing is a grandfather?	A grandpa.

Subject #4 (male)—Age: 6 years, 0 months

What is a mother?	I don't know. A mom.
Tell me all you know about mothers.	
What type of a thing is a mother?	A person. A lady.
What is a husband?	A father.
Tell me all you know about husbands.	
What type of a thing is a husband?	A person—again.
What is an aunt?	A grandma.
Tell me all you know about aunts.	
What type of a thing is an aunt?	A person. They have to be persons.
What is a sister?	Oooh. A person. A girl.
Tell me all you know about sisters.	They help you do stuff. Like doing tricks.
What type of a thing is a sister?	A person. A girl.
What is a father?	Oooh. A dad.
Tell me all you know about fathers.	I don't know. They're sometimes nice to children. They give spankings on your butt.
What type of a thing is a father?	A person.
What is a son?	Me.

Subject #4 (continued)

Tell me all you know about sons.	I do nice things to sisters. Sometimes. But not all the times.
What type of a thing is a son?	A person. I don't really know about me.
What is a grandmother?	Oooh. A grandma.
Tell me all you know about grandmothers.	They're nice. They sometimes give toys.
What type of a thing is a grandmother?	Oooh. A person—if I said an animal I would be wrong.
What is an uncle?	Some cider will help me think. I do not know about uncles.
Tell me all you know about uncles.	They're nice, nice, nice.
What type of a thing is an uncle?	A person.
What is a wife?	A mom. Cuz she's a wife. She got married.
Tell me all you know about wives.	They're nice too. Everybody's nice in my family.
What type of a thing is a wife?	A person.
What is a brother?	A son.
Tell me all you know about brothers.	Nice too.
What type of a thing is a brother?	A person. Everything's a person.
What is a daughter?	A sister.
Tell me all you know about daughters.	I've never had one—if I had one, I would know.
What type of a thing is a daughter?	A person.

What is a grandfather?	Oooh. They're a grandpa.
Tell me all you know about grandfathers.	I don't really know. My mind has to take a rest and watch TV.
What type of a thing is a grandfather?	A person.

Subject #5 (male)—Age: 7 years, 2 months

What is a mother?	A lady who gets born and has a child.
Tell me all you know about mothers.	Mothers have kids. Mothers—what's that word? Mothers—they get married.
What type of a thing is a mother?	A human or a mammal. A lady who asks you questions.
What is a husband?	It is your mom's—it is who your mom got married to.
Tell me all you know about husbands.	They're your daddy. They live in the same house and have rings too.
What type of a thing is a husband?	A man that goes golfing. Not too often though.
What is an aunt?	An aunt is your mommy or daddy's sister.
Tell me all you know about aunts.	Aunts have children and sometimes they're your mommy—they're always your mommy. Can aunts have children? Yea, they can, but they can't be your mom.
What type of a thing is an aunt?	A lady that sometimes has children.

111

Subject #5 (continued)

What is a sister?	Your mom's daughter.
Tell me all you know about sisters.	I have not that many answers because I don't have any sisters. They can be big or small, older or younger.
What type of a thing is a sister?	A mammal.
What is a father?	Your mom's husband.
Tell me all you know about fathers.	They know a lot more history than children do and they can be the president.
What type of a thing is a father?	A man that knows a lot about soccer.
What is a son?	A son? Your mom's boy.
Tell me all you know about sons.	They like to play sports sometimes and they can have glasses.
What type of a thing is a son?	What do you think? A mammal.
What is a grandmother?	Your mom's mom.
Tell me all you know about grandmothers.	Um. They're usually in their 60's.
What type of a thing is a grandmother?	A woman.
What is an uncle?	Your mom's daddy—don't write down that! Your dad's brother sometimes or always—it's always.
Tell me all you know about uncles.	My uncle Norman used to play football. My uncle Tom used to play football with my daddy. Those are facts about my uncles.

Subject #5 (continued)

What type of a thing is an uncle?	Someone who likes sports.
What is a wife?	Who your dad is married to.
Tell me all you know about wives.	They like to play with their kids. Sometimes they don't have kids. They're married to your dad.
What type of a thing is a wife?	A lady.
What is a brother?	A brother is your mom's other son.
Tell me all you know about brothers.	They're boys. They can be older or younger.
What type of a thing is a brother?	A mammal. It's a boy.
What is a daughter?	Your mom's child or your mom's son's sister.
Tell me all you know about daughters.	They're girls. They usually have long hair - usually blond to light brown.
What type of a thing is a daughter?	A mammal that's a girl.
What is a grandfather?	A grandpa? Your mom's dad.
Tell me all you know about grandfathers.	They're about the same age as your grandma. They like to go shopping—*my* grandpa does.
What type of a thing is a grandfather?	A man that's a mammal and usually in his 50's or 60's.

Subject #6 (female)—Age: 8 years, 8 months

What is a mother?	Your grandma and grandpa's daughter.
Tell me all you know about mothers.	They feed us, and help with homework—I don't have any today by the way.
What type of a thing is a mother?	A human being.
What is a husband?	Your mom's—oh—who your mom married.
Tell me all you know about husbands.	They're your father and they're nice and they help you sometimes. They play with you most of the time.
What type of a thing is a husband?	A human being.
What is an aunt?	Oh. I know this one. Your mom or dad's sister.
Tell me all you know about aunts.	O.K. They are nice and they're your cousin's mom and your uncle's wives.
What type of a thing is an aunt?	A human being.
What is a sister?	This is easy. It's your—how do I explain myself? I can't get these "what is" questions.
Tell me all you know about sisters.	They're nice. They help around the house. I help take care of the pets. What else do I do? I play with Ethan and you (mom) a lot.
What type of a thing is a sister?	A human being.
What is a father?	Your grandma and grandpa's son.

Tell me all you know about fathers.	They play with the kids a lot. They help you (mom) around the house a lot when you're busy studying. I know something he's doing right now. He's washing the car.
What type of a thing is a father?	A human being.
What is a son?	Your—like your mom and dad's boy kind of.
Tell me all you know about sons.	Let's see . . . most of the time they like to play cars and trucks and Ethan likes to play outside a lot and he likes to play on the computer—he's stuck on it.
What type of a thing is a son?	A human being.
What is a grandmother?	O.K. Your grandpa's wife. Your mom or dad's mom.
Tell me all you know about grandmothers.	They're very nice. When you visit them they're really—they help you and stuff.
What type of a thing is a grandmother?	A human being.
What is an uncle?	Your mom or dad's brother.
Tell me all you know about uncles.	They're nice.
What type of a thing is an uncle?	A human being.
What is a wife?	You're—a person that your dad married.
Tell me all you know about wives.	Well they're—I think I answered this with "mothers". They help with homework and they feed you.

Subject #6 (continued)

What type of a thing is a wife?	A human being.
What is a brother?	Your mom and dad's son.
Tell me all you know about brothers.	They're kind of wild. They like to play wild games smashing trucks and stuff. They like to play with their friends in the yard.
What type of a thing is a brother?	A monkey—no no! A human being.
What is a daughter?	Your mom and dad's daugh—sis—girl.
Tell me all you know about daughters.	They're nice and kind and help around the house. Sometimes they play with their other siblings and sometimes they help cook.
What type of a thing is a daughter?	A human being.
What is a grandfather?	Oh. Your mom or dad's father.
Tell me all you know about grandfathers.	They're nice. They talk to your father a lot and sometimes they help around the house.
What type of a thing is a grandfather?	A human being.

Parent Questionnaire

Child: Subject #1 (female)—Age: 3 years, 5 months

	My child does not have a relative of this type	My child has such a relative but has never seen him/her	My child has such a relative but seldom sees him/her	My child has such a relative and sees him/her often
father				✔
mother				✔
sister	✔			
brother				✔
aunt				✔
uncle				✔
grandmother				✔
grandfather				✔

	My child has heard this term spoken	My child has spoken this term him/herself
daughter	✔	
son	✔	
wife	✔	
husband		

Place a check mark in the column that best describes your child's experience/familiarity with each of the 12 relatives listed.

Parent Questionnaire

Child: Subject #2 (male)—Age: 3 years, 7 months

Place a check mark in the column that best describes your child's experience/familiarity with each of the 12 relatives listed.

	My child does not have a relative of this type	My child has such a relative but has never seen him/her	My child has such a relative but seldom sees him/her	My child has such a relative and sees him/her often
father				✔
mother				✔
sister	✔			
brother				✔
aunt				✔
uncle				✔
grandmother				✔
grandfather				✔

	My child has heard this term spoken	My child has spoken this term him/herself
daughter		
son	✔	
wife	✔	
husband	✔	

Parent Questionnaire

Child: Subject #3 (female)—Age: 5 years, 6 months

	My child does not have a relative of this type	My child has such a relative but has never seen him/her	My child has such a relative but seldom sees him/her	My child has such a relative and sees him/her often
father				✓
mother				✓
sister				✓
brother				✓
aunt			✓	
uncle			✓	
grandmother				✓
grandfather				✓

	My child has heard this term spoken	My child has spoken this term him/herself
daughter	✓	✓
son	✓	✓
wife	✓	✓
husband	✓	✓

Place a check mark in the column that best describes your child's experience/familiarity with each of the 12 relatives listed.

Parent Questionnaire

Child: Subject #4 (male)—Age: 6 years, 0 months

	My child does not have a relative of this type	My child has such a relative but has never seen him/her	My child has such a relative but seldom sees him/her	My child has such a relative and sees him/her often
father				✔
mother				✔
sister				✔
brother	✔			
aunt				✔
uncle				✔
grandmother				✔
grandfather				✔

	My child has heard this term spoken	My child has spoken this term him/herself
daughter	✔	✔
son	✔	✔
wife	✔	✔
husband	✔	✔

Place a check mark in the column that best describes your child's experience/familiarity with each of the 12 relatives listed.

Parent Questionnaire

Child: Subject #5 (male)—Age: 7 years, 2 months

	My child does not have a relative of this type	My child has such a relative but has never seen him/her	My child has such a relative but seldom sees him/her	My child has such a relative and sees him/her often
father				✓
mother				✓
sister	✓			
brother	✓			
aunt				✓
uncle				✓
grandmother				✓
grandfather				✓

	My child has heard this term spoken	My child has spoken this term him/herself
daughter	✓	✓
son	✓	✓
wife	✓	✓
husband	✓	✓

Place a check mark in the column that best describes your child's experience/familiarity with each of the 12 relatives listed.

Parent Questionnaire

Child: Subject #3 (male)—Age: 6 years, 0 months

	My child does not have a relative of this type	My child has such a relative but has never seen him/her	My child has such a relative but seldom sees him/her	My child has such a relative and sees him/her often
father				✓
mother				✓
sister	✓			
brother				✓
aunt				✓
uncle				✓
grandmother				✓
grandfather				✓

	My child has heard this term spoken	My child has spoken this term him/herself
daughter	✓	✓
son	✓	✓
wife	✓	✓
husband	✓	

Place a check mark in the column that best describes your child's experience/familiarity with each of the 12 relatives listed.